"A Counterpoint of Dissonance"

"A Counterpoint of Dissonance"

The Aesthetics and Poetry of Gerard Manley Hopkins

Michael Sprinker

The Johns Hopkins University Press
Baltimore and London

This book has been brought to publication with the generous assistance of Oregon State University.

The Johns Hopkins University Press, Baltimore, Maryland 21218
The Johns Hopkins Press Ltd., London

Library of Congress Cataloging in Publication Data

Sprinker, Michael.
    A counterpoint of dissonance.

    1. Hopkins, Gerard Manley, 1844-1889—Criticism and interpretation. 2. Hopkins, Gerard Manley, 1844-1889—Aesthetics. I. Title.
PR4803.H44Z848 1980   821'.8   80-13585
ISBN 0-8018-2402-8

For Erich Heller

CONTENTS

ACKNOWLEDGMENTS

IN ANY INTELLECTUAL UNDERTAKING, one incurs many more debts than he can possibly discharge in the short space allotted for acknowledgments. Nonetheless, certain obligations incurred during the research and writing of the present book deserve mention. Though I had encountered the joys (and the painful difficulties) of Hopkins's verse as an undergraduate, my serious interest in Hopkins first took shape under the tutelage of Professor Robert Martin in his graduate seminar on Victorian poetry. It was he who encouraged my early sallies against that forbidding "dragon in the gate," and since then his continuing enthusiasm for my work has been of inestimable value. I also owe a special debt of gratitude to Professor Hans Aarsleff, who read an early version of my second chapter on Hopkins's theory of language and recommended it for publication. His vast and detailed knowledge of the history of linguistics and his painstaking corrections of my many amateurish errors clarified much that was fuzzy in my own thinking and gave much-needed encouragement to the interpretive project on Hopkins that eventually issued from this study of the problem of language theory in the nineteenth century. For careful readings of earlier versions of the entire manuscript and for helpful suggestions for improving it, I am grateful to Professors James Olney, A. Walton Litz, and J. Hillis Miller. My considerable debt to Professor Miller's seminal study of Hopkins in *The Disappearance of God* and to his more recent writings on Hopkins and on literary theory have, I hope, been made manifest in the course of the book. It is characteristic of his generosity and stature as a scholar that he has continued to encourage and support my work despite the rather different conclusions to which each of us has come in our study of the same texts.

At various stages during research and writing, I have benefited from the financial support of the following institutions: the Research Council, the College of Liberal Arts, and the English Department of Oregon State University; the National Endowment for the Humanities; and the Society for the Humanities at Cornell University. Without their generous aid, I should certainly not have completed this project so expeditiously.

I wish also to thank Professor Philip Wiener of the *Journal of the History of Ideas* for permission to reprint a portion of chapter 2 which originally appeared in that journal.

For typing and proofreading assistance, I am indebted to Betty Slater, Cheryl Schlappi, Anne-Marie Garcia, Philip Garrett, and John Kitzmiller. The editorial ministrations of Mary Lou Kenney and Carrie McKee have made the difficult task of transforming a manuscript into a book a genuine pleasure.

Much that I have written has been encouraged and helpfully criticized by my colleagues in the English department at Oregon State University. Many of the disagreements about method in which they and I have engaged have helped to clarify my thinking for the present book. I especially wish to thank Richard Daniels, whose perpetual goodwill and thoughtful criticism have kept alive the spark of intellectual curiosity and commitment without which no scholarly labor can long survive.

Finally, to my wife, Kristy, I am indebted in so many ways that to try to thank her here can only be an embarrassment. Her continuing support as typist, editor, and spiritual guide have made my work and my life rewarding and fulfilling. To her are due my deepest feelings of gratitude and love. I hope this book may serve as partial recompense for her unwavering commitment to its coming into being.

"A Counterpoint of Dissonance"

Key to Abbreviations

The following abbreviations are cited parenthetically throughout to identify Hopkins's writings:

P   *The Poems of Gerard Manley Hopkins*, ed. W. H. Gardner and N. H. Mackenzie, 4th edition (London: Oxford University Press, 1967).

J   *The Journals and Papers of Gerard Manley Hopkins*, ed., Humphry House and Graham Storey (London: Oxford University Press, 1959).

S   *The Sermons and Devotional Writings of Gerard Manley Hopkins*, ed. Christopher Devlin, S.J. (London: Oxford University Press, 1959).

L. I   *The Letters of Gerard Manley Hopkins to Robert Bridges*, ed. Claude Colleer Abbott (London: Oxford University Press, 1955).

L. II   *The Correspondence of Gerard Manley Hopkins and Richard Watson Dixon*, ed. Claude Colleer Abbott (London: Oxford University Press, 1955).

L. III   *Further Letters of Gerard Manley Hopkins, Including His Correspondence with Coventry Patmore*, ed. Claude Colleer Abbott, 2nd edition, rev. and enl. (London: Oxford University Press, 1956).

INTRODUCTION

As ANYONE EVEN SLIGHTLY ACQUAINTED with the current dialogue (or *poly-logues*, to borrow Julia Kristéva's term) in literary criticism knows, writing an introduction (or preface) is no longer as simple or straightforward an act as it once seemed to be. Derrida (and not only him) has made one's confession of the *post-scriptum* nature of a preface virtually obligatory. But in the present case, the matter can be approached somewhat differently. Though the sentences I am presently composing are in fact written after the completion of the rest of the manuscript, what will follow shortly was written *in medias res*, about two-thirds of the way through the writing of the rough draft, if memory serves.

I originally intended to include my reading of "The Windhover" as a separate chapter between the ones on "The Wreck of the Deutschland" and the last poems. I now offer it here as a specimen of the strategy of reading I have chosen to solicit meanings from Hopkins's writings. To an audience steeped in the idioms of poststructuralism, much that I shall say will sound all too familiar, though I submit Hopkins as a particularly apt instance of the grammatological double bind exposed by Derrida—a sort of "Victorian Mallarmé," as one reader remarked about a preliminary version of the present argument. To an audience either not initiated into the "mysteries of deconstruction" or to one informed about but still resistant to "la marche derridienne," what follows may appear harsh or dogmatic, even sterile. To these readers, I can only respond by saying that harshness and sterility, and even a certain dogmatism, are the very themes in Hopkins that strike me as most important, as the same themes struck Valéry as those most characteristic of Mallarmé, and that my reading of Hopkins attempts to solicit this aspect of his texts and to liberate those texts from the weight of a critical tradition that has rendered them more or less innocuous—"sivilized" them, as Huck Finn would say. I have couched my reading of "The Windhover" in the most extreme terms possible (for me at least), not merely for the sake of polemics, but in the belief that only through such a strong reading can this text—and others—attain a free standing among the great lyrics written in English, for it is just such extremity that "The Windhover"—and all of Hopkins's writings—proposes as the necessary condition of poetry. I begin with a quotation (originally the epigraph to the chapter I intended) from Harold

Bloom, the exemplary relation of which to the poem and my reading will, I trust, become obvious as my text unfolds.

. . . a poem both takes its origin in a Scene of Instruction and finds its necessary aim or purpose there as well. It is only by repressing creative "freedom," through the initial fixation of influence, that a person can be reborn as a poet. And only by revising that repression can a poet become and remain strong. Poetry, revisionism, and repression verge upon a melancholy identity, an identity that is broken afresh by every new strong poem, and mended afresh by the same poem.
                                    —Harold Bloom, *Poetry and Repression*

Among the innumerable commentaries on "The Windhover," none, so far as I am aware, has recognized in this poem an allegory of the writing of poetry. There have been many elucidations of the poem's allegorical elements, and there have been almost as many readings of the poem as a representation of Hopkins's personal crisis as a poet. But no reading has brought together the two strains of interpretive strategy that would read the poem as a figural presentation of poetic figuration, a powerful rhetorical statement about the burden and the inevitability of rhetoric. Those commentators who have labeled the poem autobiographical do not go far enough, for the poem is indeed an autobiography, though less of the empirical, historical self of the poet than of the poetic identity that is and can only be realized in the writing of the poem itself. As he did even more grandiosely in "The Wreck of the Deutschland," Hopkins creates himself as poet in this poem, though in the paradoxical, antithetical mode peculiar to poetry in which creation is inseparable from destruction. Hopkins becomes a poet in "The Windhover" by a phoenix-like act of self-immolation; from the ashes of the empirical self emerges the renewed self of the poet.

The recent work of Harold Bloom provides for me the most powerful and compelling elaboration of the poet's struggle to identity through the writing of poems.[1] The separation of the poetic self from the empirical self is, Bloom argues, the dominant force in all poets since Milton, and in saying so Bloom is not alone. Compare, for example, Erich Heller's

[1]See Harold Bloom, *The Anxiety of Influence* (New York: Oxford University Press, 1973); idem, *A Map of Misreading* (New York: Oxford University Press, 1975); idem, *Kabbalah and Criticism* (New York: Seabury Press, 1975); idem, *Poetry and Repression* (New Haven: Yale University Press, 1976).

description (strongly influenced, as is Bloom's theory of poetry, by Nietzsche) of the "lyrical I" of the modern poet:

> The "I" of the successful lyrical poem is not identical with the empirico-biographical "I" of the poet. In the act of poetic creation it frees itself, Nietzsche writes, of his individual will and turns itself into a mere medium, in which and through which it finds its redemption by contemplating and uttering the *idea* of itself. . . . Through the poem the poet's self becomes an "aesthetic phenomenon," as Nietzsche calls it in *The Birth of Tragedy*, saying of it that it is the *only justification* of world and existence, and now, by implication, also of the human person. . . . The "I" of the poem, as subject *and* object of lyrical contemplation, begins to speak only when the "merely"-human "I" has come to an end.[2]

This realization of poetic selfhood, for both Bloom and Heller, is perishable and must be renewed with each lyrical moment. As Bloom puts it, poetic identity "is broken afresh by every new strong poem, and mended afresh by the same poem." The more pronounced fragility of this identity among modern poets in comparison to their classical ancestors is the sad central motif of both Heller's and Bloom's work, and it is the increasing fragility of Hopkins's poetic identity as his career progressed that I wish to reveal.

"The Windhover" begins by posing this very problem, the meaning of the "lyrical I." Who or what is the "I" that announces itself in the poem's first word? And what is signified by "caught"? "Caught a glimpse of" seems an obvious reading, but the sense of "capture" lingers in the background. Perhaps seeing (perceiving) and possessing do not, as Geoffrey Hartman has suggested, entirely conflict: "So thing and perceiver, thing and actor, tend in the sight of Hopkins to be joined to each other as if by electrical charge; they are connected like windhover and wind in terms of stress given and received."[3] What is caught? The windhover, "morning's minion, king- / dom of daylight's dauphin, dapple-dawn-drawn Falcon." This would appear to resolve the ambiguity of "caught," since if we read the poem literally (as Paul Mariani commands us always to do with Hopkins),[4] it would be unlikely that Hopkins meant he had physically captured a kestrel. As the poem continues, this becomes

---

[2]Erich Heller, *The Poet's Self and the Poem* (London: Athlone Press, 1976), p. 24.

[3]Geoffrey Hartman, *The Unmediated Vision* (1954; rpt. New York: Harcourt, Brace & World, 1966), p. 55.

[4]Paul Mariani, *A Commentary on the Complete Poems of Gerard Manley Hopkins* (Ithaca: Cornell University Press, 1970), p. 112.

more clear, for Hopkins indicates that what he "caught" is not so much the bird itself as its actions:

> I caught this morning morning's minion, king-
> dom of daylight's dauphin, dapple-dawn-drawn Falcon, in
>   his riding
> Of the rolling level underneath him steady air, and striding
> High there, how he rung upon the rein of a wimpling wing
> In his ecstasy! then off, off forth on swing,
>   As a skate's heel sweeps smooth on a bow-bend: the
>   hurl and gliding
> Rebuffed the big wind.

It is almost as if the capturing were accomplished not by Hopkins but by the kestrel, whose flight caught and riveted the poet's attention, an experience which is recaptured in the representation of it in the poem. As Hartman argues, "thing and perceiver," bird and poet, are joined in the act of perception, so that the flight of the windhover is "caught" by Hopkins only when Hopkins is himself "caught" or arrested by the unusual form of the bird's flight.

To read the poem in this way is to take it, in the first instance, as the representation in language of a perceptual experience, a mimesis of the physical world inhabited by the poet. Though I would not deny that Hopkins had indeed observed the flight of the kestrel and that he could describe its peculiar manner of hovering in the wind very accurately, all this seems to me only the beginning of any reading of the poem. Strictly speaking, the poem is not about a bird at all, nor even about the transcriptions of a perceptual experience, though interpretation must begin with the elements and relationships posited by the poem as if it were about a physical bird and the sighting of its flight by the poet. If the bird in the poem has a referent outside the poem itself, it is not so much the kestrel as all those birds so preternaturally present in the Romantic lyric: Keats's nightingale, Shelley's skylark, Tennyson's eagle, Hardy's darkling thrush, Yeats's falcon and golden singing bird, and Stevens's blackbird. In each of these poems, the song or the flight of the bird becomes an emblem of the poet's own voice, of his vocation, in the original sense of a "calling or summons," as a poet. "The Windhover," like two other of Hopkins's poems of this period, "The Sea and the Skylark" and "The Caged Skylark," situates itself within this powerful tradition, which, along with running water, the tower or mountain peak, the wind, *et cetera*, is among the principal tropes of Romanticism. Hopkins's windhover is itself troped in the poem. The poem is thus a figurative response to the figures of Romanticism. It tropes on a trope, as Bloom would say. But Hopkins gives the further rhetorical twist, unusual among the major English Romantics, of religious orthodoxy. Keats wrote his "Ode to a Nightingale," Shelley addressed his poem "To a Skylark," but Hopkins addresses his poem "To Christ Our Lord."

All interpreters of "The Windhover" have recognized that its true subject is not the flight of the kestrel but the Incarnation and Redemption of Christ. Most have assumed that this "underthought" is the figurative meaning intended by the literal description of the bird's movements. W. H. Gardner's paraphrase of the poem is representative:

> I *inscape* this windhover as the symbol or analogue of Christ, Son of God, the supreme Chevalier. May the human equivalents of this bird's heroic graces and perfectly disciplined *physical* activity be combined and brought to a much higher *spiritual* activity in my own being, just as these attributes were once and for all so transmuted in Christ. It is the law of things that characteristic natural action or "selving," however humble it may be, frequently gives off flashes of heart-stirring beauty; how much more then should characteristically Christ-like action (including conscientious toil and willing self-sacrifice) give glory and be pleasing to Christ our Lord! [P, 267]

Gardner's interpretation shows a characteristic confusion of the literal with the figurative. The bird's flight is "literally" represented in the poem; Christ is "figuratively" represented by "the symbol or analogue" of the windhover. But in what sense can the poem be said to represent the flight of the windhover? Obviously, the bird is not physically present on the page, nor can the reader actually behold its flight. What the reader perceives are the words of the poet, which are themselves already figural. Hopkins does not say simply that he saw a hawk, a falcon, a kestrel, or a windhover (the last word is already a figurative designation for this species of bird, a metonymy derived from the kestrel's peculiar manner of flying), but that he "caught this morning morning's minion, king- / dom of daylight's dauphin, dapple-dawn-drawn Falcon." Nor does he say that he beheld a bird in flight, but "caught" "his riding" and "striding," "how he rung upon the the rein of a wimpling wing," "the hurl and gliding." Whatever perceptual experience might have preceded the writing of the poem, the poem itself presents only language; the tropes and figures of the first eight lines are taken from language, not from nature. If the poem has a literal meaning it is simply this: "I am a poem."

To paraphrase Bloom, who claims that poems are psyches represented in texts, the poem is a self presented textually in the tropes of language structured by rhythm and rhyme. To write poetry was for Hopkins an act of self-creation, or, in Hopkins's own terminology, "selving." The best gloss on "The Windhover" is thus another poem by Hopkins in which the language of the poem foregrounds the activity of selving:

> As kingfishers catch fire, dragonflies draw flame;
>> As tumbled over rim in roundy wells
>> Stones ring; like each tucked string tells, each hung bell's
> Bow swung finds tongue to fling out broad its name;
> Each mortal thing does one thing and the same:
>> Deals out that being indoors each one dwells;
>> Selves—goes itself, *myself* it speaks and spells,
> Crying *What I do is me: for that I came.*
>
> Í say more: the just man justices;
>> Keeps gráce: thát keeps all his goings graces;
> Acts in God's eye what in God's eye he is—
>> Chríst. For Christ plays in ten thousand places,
> Lovely in limbs, and lovely in eyes not his
>> To the Father through the features of man's faces. [P, 90]

If each "mortal thing" "Selves—goes itself; *myself* it speaks and spells, / Crying What I do is me: for that I came," then each poem says no more than "I am a poem, this poem, 'As kingfishers catch fire.'" But the "lyrical I" who speaks this peom and identifies himself in the sestet says more. The poem not only proclaims its own existence but also its imitation of Christ. This is not at all the same thing as saying that the poem or the "I" *is* Christ. The poem's action, represented in the figure "the just man justices," is the representation of the self in the tropes of language, the transformation of self from existent to text. This action of the poem, its selving, is a metonymy for Christ's Incarnation. Just as Christ is "worded," to take a figure from "The Wreck of the Deutschland," in the *Logos*, so the poem attains being through rhetoric; just as Christ triumphally proclaims His being in the world by His death on the cross and His Resurrection, so the poem cries out its own being by revealing itself as language, and not just any language but the troped language we designate poetry. No poem can present itself except rhetorically; no poem can say more of itself than "I am a poem."

This brings us back to the question I first posed, and which the poem itself first raises: who or what is the "I" that announces its presence at the beginning of "The Windhover" and speaks what follows? And to whom is this "I" speaking? The poem is addressed or perhaps dedicated "To Christ Our Lord." Is it He, then, who is spoken to when the "I" exclaims "O my chevalier!" and "ah my dear"? If so, what is the point of the poem? To instruct Christ in the meaning of His own sacrifice? And is there not more than a little presumption in addressing Christ as "my dear"?

These are all challenging questions, and I believe the poem proposes them to any rigorous reading. To begin to answer them, we must return to my original claim about this poem, that it is an allegory of the writing of poetry. I understand allegory in the following way. Allegorical art originates in what we might today call an excess of the signified.[5] This is to say that the allegorical sign is produced by a heterogeneity between sign and referent, between word and thing. The value of the allegorical sign arises in an act of interpretation in which the interpreter—the poet or the reader of the poem—relates one allegorical sign to another. The value of the sign is thus determined by its relationship to other signs rather than to anything outside the signifying structure of which it is a part. As Walter Benjamin instructs us concerning the allegorical art of the baroque German drama, the purpose of allegory "is not so much to unveil material objects as to strip them naked. The emblematist does not present the essence implicitly, 'behind the image.' He drags the essence of what is depicted out before the image, in writing, as a caption, such as, in the emblem-books, forms an intimate part of what is depicted."[6] Alle-

---

[5]In characterizing allegory thus, I am indebted to the work of Thomas Weiskel, whose essay, *The Romantic Sublime* (Baltimore: Johns Hopkins University Press, 1976), draws upon Roman Jakobson's monograph, *Two Aspects of Language and Two Types of Aphasic Disturbances*, to distinguish between two versions of the semantic discontinuity he calls the Romantic sublime: the metaphorical or reader's sublime, and the metonymical or poet's sublime. The former indicates an excess of the signifier (the reader asks: what can all these signs mean? what can all these words and phrases in a poem signify?); the latter indicates an excess of the signified (each word or phrase can mean virtually anything). Weiskel is careful to point out that the distinction between reader and poet is not absolute, since all readers create the significances in poems as if they were poets while reading, and all poets are readers when they organize the chaotic significations of language into poems. In Weiskel's terms, allegory would be a poetic activity in which metonymy predominates. Allegorical signs are metonymies rather than metaphors.

Paul de Man's recent work, *Allegories of Reading* (New Haven: Yale University Press, 1979), appeared too late for me to integrate a thorough discussion of his rigorous theoretical meditation on allegory into my reading of "The Windhover." I may just indicate here, however, that his description of the necessary anacoluthon or parabasis in allegorical narratives could be instructively compared with my discussion of the function of the word "buckle" in "The Windhover," (see *Allegories of Reading*, p. 300, and below pp. 13-14), and that his theorizing of the textual machine of deconstruction (see *Allegories of Reading*, p. 298) would further illuminate the themes of self, language, figure, and text that recur throughout the present essay on Hopkins.

[6]Walter Benjamin, *Ursprung des deutschen Trauerspiels*, trans. John Osborne, *The Origin of German Tragic Drama* (London: New Left Books, 1977), p. 185.

gorical art foregrounds the signifying process. It forces the signifying structure of the allegorical script upon the reader's attention and deflects any attempt by the reader to interpret the allegorical sign as a representation of something beyond the allegory itself. Allegory thus arises from and produces in the reader a "deep-rooted intuition of the problematic character of art."[7]

The interpretive problems presented by "The Windhover" derive from its allegorical structure. As I have suggested, it simply will not do to refer the imagery of the poem back to some perceptual experience of the flight of the kestrel, for the language of the poem is irreducibly figural and does not originate in a physical event in nature. "Morning's minion, king- / dom of daylight's dauphin" and all the other representations of the windhover in the poem are tropes which cannot refer to or be interpreted by referring to any species of bird in nature. Neither does the figure of Christ which lurks in the background of the poem's imagery ("dauphin," "ecstasy," "chevalier," "gall," "gash") resolve the poem's language into a fixed and invariant system of meanings arranged in a hierarchy (as the reading of Gardner and most other allegorists seeks to establish). Each of the words reminding the reader of the presence of Christ in the poem is itself a figural, not a literal, image of the Redemption. Christ is the Prince of Peace, and thus the word "dauphin" in the second line can be assigned a value that inserts the figure of Christ into the poem's signifying structure, but this only by a metonymic subsitution, since Prince of Peace is only one of Christ's attributes and not His true or complete being.

Moreover, much of the poem cannot be referred back to Christ as the interpretive key to the poem's significations. The word "chevalier," for instance, can be understood as an indication of Christ as soldier/knight, a commonplace in Jesuit spirituality instilled in Hopkins by his making the *Spiritual Exercises*. Its peculiar appropriateness to the poem, however, is determined by a series of equestrian figures that have no bearing on or particular reference to Christian iconography: "striding / High," "rung upon the rein," "shéer plód makes plough down sillion / Shine." The figure of Christ as chevalier does not determine the value of these phrases, any more than they determine the value of Christ's knighthood, but both taken together produce a signifying structure in which Christ, kestrel, poet, horse, and much else are elements whose value fluctuates with the differing juxtapositions that the poet and reader make among them. Any

[7]Ibid., p. 176.

reader must make appeals to other signifying structures outside the poem, such as Christian iconography, particularly in its Jesuit form, Shakespeare's *Henry V*—which is where Gardner locates the origin of "dauphin" and the images of the horse (see P, 267), falconry, skating; but none of these structures can be designated as primary or absolutely determinate for the poem's meaning.

It is only within the poem itself, in the play of the various figures derived from these other signifying structures, that the signs taken from elsewhere can be assigned a determinate value, and then only in the sense that the value of each sign is determined by the signifying structure of the poem which the sign itself goes to produce. In other words, there can be no final, unchanging meaning for the poem. What the poem intends is an allegorical structure constituted by a repetition of signs in a relationship of temporal difference in which meaning is a perpetually deferred event, for any meaning that might be attached to the allegorical sign depends not only on those signs which precede and succeed the allegorical sign itself but also on the alteration in value it will effect in those other signs. As Paul de Man has correctly said, "allegory designates primarily a distance in relation to its own origin, and, renouncing the nostalgia and the desire to coincide, it establishes its language in the void of this temporal difference."[8] An allegorical poem like "The Windhover" displays meaning as an historical event that is not part of a continuum but exists as a moment in a dispersion or field of events capable of being crystallized momentarily by the tracing of certain lines of force through the field. These lines of force are the interpretive strategies suggested by the text and deployed by the reader, but such strategies specifically lack any hierarchical principles by which one pattern can be said to control all the others. Allegory signifies the incapacity of the text to be controlled, dominated, or explained by any single reading or any synthesis of several readings; it is the dance or play of interpretation as unrestricted economy.[9]

[8] Paul de Man, "The Rhetoric of Temporality," in *Interpretation*, ed. Charles S. Singleton (Baltimore: Johns Hopkins University Press, 1969), p. 191.

[9] See Jacques Derrida, "From Restricted to General Economy," in *Writing and Difference*, trans. Alan Bass (Chicago: University of Chicago Press, 1978), pp. 251-77. It should be emphasized that allegory does not eliminate a representational language entirely, that is, allegory does not simply negate the level of interpretation on which, for example, a reader of "The Windhover" would note the correspondences between the language of the poem and the flight of the kestrel hawk. Allegory always intends representation, in the sense of a language which refers to events, objects, or creatures in the physical world, but at the same time it always discovers the incapacity of language to represent anything other than itself. This aspect of allegory has been neatly summarized by Paul de Man: "All representational poetry is always also allegorical, whether it be aware of it or not, and the allegorical power

We are brought back once again to my original question: Who or what is the "I" that opens the poem, and what has this "I" "caught"? Briefly, the "I" is the poet, not the empirico-biographical person Gerard Manley Hopkins, but the "lyrical I." It is the poet as he creates himself as poet in the unfolding of the text. What the poet "catches" (the pun on the noun form—"catch" as song or tune—is, I believe, certainly submerged in the text, an example of Empson's "second type of ambiguity")[10] is the figurative play of language achieved in the poem. In this way, the windhover *is* the poem; the figurative flight of the bird described in the first ten lines is an allegorical representation of the poet's own struggle with language in writing poetry. Insofar as the poem is realized, insofar as it becomes the poem that the poet is speaking, it achieves and masters the flight of figurative language. "The achieve of, the mastery of the thing!" is the poet's exclamation of his desire to create the poem, to master the tropes of language that are so admirable and seemingly inimitable in themselves. Having attained this plateau of self-consciousness, knowing that the object of his desire is the already achieved mastery of figure, the poet turns back upon himself to reflect upon the means of this mastery. Having "caught" the windhover in the octet, the poet reproduces the

---

of the language undermines and obscures the specific literal meaning of a representation open to understanding. But all allegorical poetry must contain a representational element that invites and allows for understanding, only to discover that the understanding it reaches is necessarily in error" (De Man, "Lyric and Modernity," in *Blindness and Insight* [New York: Oxford University Press, 1971], p. 185). The continuing intention of Hopkins's poetry was this quest for understanding; its tragedy was the discovery that all such understanding was "necessarily in error." As in Aristotle's conception of the highest form of tragedy (*Poetics*, XI. 3-4), *anagnorisis* and *peripateia* coincide.

[10]See *Seven Types of Ambiguity*, 3rd ed. (1953; rpt. Harmondsworth: Penguin Books, 1961), chapter 2. Empson subsequently discusses "The Windhover" as an example of his seventh type of ambiguity, which "occurs when the two meanings of the word, the two values of the ambiguity, are the two opposite meanings defined by the context, so that the total effect is to show a fundamental division in the writer's mind" (p. 225). Empson's analysis, which he takes from I. A. Richards, concludes that there is an irresolvable tension in the poem between the active life of the windhover and the spiritual life of the Jesuit poet: "Confronted suddenly with the active physical beauty of the bird, he conceives it as the opposite of his patient spiritual renunciation; the statements of the poem appear to insist that his own life is superior, but he cannot decisively judge between them, and holds both with agony in his mind" (p. 261). My disagreements with this reading of the poem will be evident as my own reading proceeds, though it should be obvious that I believe Empson's and Richards's opposition of the "physical beauty of the bird" to Hopkins's "patient spiritual renunciation" to be a false one. That this opposition would be powerfully figured in the poems Hopkins was to write a decade later does not alter the fact that in "The Windhover" the poet's succesful imitation of Christ is not only celebrated but is in fact accomplished in the poem. There is, I believe, a temporal curve to Hopkins's poetic career that the extreme formalism of the Empson-Richards interpretation simply elides.

manner of his catching in the sestet. In these six lines, some of the most quoted and indeed most beautiful in modern poetry, Hopkins allegorizes his own poetic destiny by doubling the poem back upon itself to reflect the process of its own making:

> Brute beauty and valour and act, oh, air, pride, plume, here
> > Buckle! AND the fire that breaks from thee then, a billion
> Times told lovelier, more dangerous, O my chevalier!
>
> > No wonder of it: shéer plód makes plough down sillion
> Shine, and blue-bleak embers, ah my dear,
> > Fall, gall themselves, and gash gold-vermilion.

All commentators agree that the interpretive crux of the poem is the word "Buckle," and many have noted that the poem does precisely what this word proclaims at the point where it occurs in the poem—it collapses only to rise again transfigured. Once again, Gardner is the best guide to to the interpretive difficulties presented by this word:

> This presumably imperative (but possibly indicative) vb. is the main crux of the poem. Which of three possible meanings did the poet intend? Each one has been regarded, by *some* commentators, as exclusively or primarily apposite: (1) the arch. "prepare for action," "come to grips," "engage the enemy"; (2) "clasp, enclose, fasten together" as under one discipline; (3) the more common meanings, "bend, crumple up, collapse" under weight or strain. Meaning (2) is clearly implied in ll. 1-8—the bird's controlled flight; (1) makes the militant kestrel-hawk the symbol of the Christian knight valiantly warring against evil, and is supported by the chivalric imagery—"dauphin," "riding," "rein"; (3) suggests the abnegation of "mortal beauty" (cf. No. 62) and the readiness to suffer and be immolated. In its complex "discipline-flight-fall" meanings and connotation, *Buckle!* links the joyful panache and mastery of the octave to the poignant yet triumphant resignation of "Fáll, gáll themselves, &c." of l. 14. As a Jesuit, G.M.H. meditated regularly on the Kingship and soldiership of Christ (see the *Spiritual Exercises* of St. Ignatius Loyola, and poems Nos. 63 and 73) and on His Crucifixion; he was also deeply concerned with his own personal and vocational "Imitation of Christ." [P, 267-68]

Gardner's commentary admirably summarizes the principal critical positions with respect to the poem, and he quite rightly tries to show that all three meanings of "Buckle!" can be sustained in a single interpretation.

But Gardner fails to recognize what for me remains the most compelling implication of his own reasoning, namely, that the "personal and vocational 'Imitation of Christ'" which he correctly identifies as the subject of the poem is accomplished only in the act of poetic creation. The poem is not a meditation, as silent prayer would be, but a textual realization of the mystery of Christ's suffering. The struggle of the poet with figurative language and the signifying structures bequeathed to him by tradition is dramatized in the figural representations of the flight of the windhover and the Crucifixion and Resurrection of Christ. The powerful *askesis* of Christ's Incarnation and Crucifixion is doubled in the image of the bird's apparent collapse in flight, and both are figural representations of the poet's own *askesis* necessary to the creation of the poem. The flight of the windhover does not present a forbidding image of physical grace antithetical to the poet's "hidden" spiritual crusade, but rather, by its figural hovering in the first nine lines and its fall in line ten, the poem brings forth the paradoxical triumph through limitation that is Christ's peculiar achievement and the poet's destiny. By an act of willed limitation, the poet, like Christ, blazes forth in greater glory, his poetic "fire" shines "a billion / Times told lovelier, more dangerous." Most of all, it is the diligent labor, the repetition over and over again of the familiar tropes and figures inherited from tradition that give this poem its special power to move us. Hopkins's "shéer plód" over the ground of conventional language and religious imagery, his stirring of the "blue-bleak embers" of English Romantic poetry and of the traditions of Catholic spirituality, make his own poetic plough shine and cause those dying embers of tradition to "gash gold-vermilion." The fallen world of nineteenth-century poetry and post-medieval Catholicism gives impetus to this poem, but the poet himself produces the glorious burst of energy that precedes the utter collapse of tradition into complete skepticism and nihilism. As Benjamin has wisely remarked, allegory originates in the Fall of Man: "The triumph of subjectivity and the onset of an arbitrary rule over things, is the origin of all allegorical contemplation. In the very fall of man the unity of guilt and signifying emerges as an abstraction. The allegorical has its existence in abstractions; as an abstraction, as a faculty of the spirit of language itself, it is at home in the Fall."[11]

Poised on the edge of the abyss, allegory maintains its precarious equilibrium at a severe price, for the poet's Christ-like resurrection in his poem is achieved only through the most strenuous linguistic somersaults.

[11]Walter Benjamin, *The Origin of German Tragic Drama*, pp. 233-34.

Finally, the strain of maintaining his balance became too great for Hopkins, as the increasingly evident despair in his late poems and letters shows. The glorious fire that breaks forth in "The Windhover" was gradually extinguished by the growing frigidity of Hopkins's poetic life, which ended with the mournful sestet of his last poem, "To R. B.":

> Sweet fire the sire of muse, my soul needs this;
> I want the one rapture of an inspiration.
> O then if in my lagging lines you miss
>
> The roll, the rise, the carol, the creation,
> My winter world, that scarcely breathes that bliss
> Now, yields you, with some sighs, our explanation. [P, 108]

This is perhaps the place to say a few more preliminary words about the critical project attempted in my interpretation of Hopkins's writings and my tracing of the arc of his career as a poet. It is certainly the place to comment upon the scope of the terms "modern" and "modernism," which I employ at various times in what follows to locate Hopkins, more precisely than he has been in the past, on the continuum of literary history, specifically within the post-Miltonic tradition of the Sublime in English poetry. What is meant and what is at stake when I say, at the end of this essay, that with Hopkins "modern English poetry properly begins"?

To begin to answer this question, I turn to a seemingly unlikely source for interpreting modern English poetry: Walter Benjamin's essay, "The Paris of the Second Empire in Baudelaire." My choice is doubly unlikely in that Benjamin nowhere, so far as I know, discusses Hopkins (in fact, he rarely treats English poetry at all), and also in that this particular essay, a portion of his never completed "Arcades Project," specifically concerns the relation of the writer (Baudelaire) to the political and social conditions of his time (the middle decades of the nineteenth century), a relation that I have, for strategic reasons, omitted in my own interpretation of Hopkins. But the finest insights, as Hopkins knew, often arise in unlikely places and appear at "unforeseen times rather—as skies / Betweenpie mountains" (P, 103). As an exemplary figure for the modern poet, Baudelaire stood in Benjamin's eyes for the enormous effort demanded of the poet-laborer in modern society. Benjamin achieves this insight with some difficulty, since Baudelaire went to great lengths to hide his own laborious struggles with language, glorifying in his poetry the figures of the bohemian, the dandy, and the flâneur—figures all the very antithesis of the sweat and sacrifice Benjamin associates with Baudelaire the poet. At stake in this interpretation for Benjamin is the demystification of the bourgeois cult of genius, the energetic denial that there is some occult power or innate ability that makes one man more creative than another.

According to Benjamin, it is not genius that makes the modern poet, but agonized work, the achievement of freedom in the face of the most daunting obstacles. Hence, for Benjamin, the central figure of modernism is the hero:

> The hero is the true subject of modernism. In other words, it takes a heroic constitution to live modernism. That was also Balzac's opinion. With their belief, Balzac and Baudelaire are in opposition to Romanticism. They transfigure passions and resolution; the Romanticists transfigured renunciation and surrender.[12]

But this heroic figure who haunts Baudelaire's lines and Balzac's narratives is no Napoleonic strongman, even less is he an *Übermensch*. Modernism is not the realization of the heroic, but the doomed quest for the hero, the playing of the hero's part and the discovery that the mantle no longer fits. Commenting on Baudelaire's fascination with the image of ships at anchor, Benjamin says:

> In the ships, nonchalance is combined with readiness for the utmost exertion of energy. This gives them a secret significance. There is a special constellation in which greatness and indolence meet in human beings, too. This constellation governed Baudelaire's life. He deciphered it and called it "modernism." When he loses himself to the spectacle of the ships lying at anchor, he does so in order to derive an allegory from them. The hero is as strong, as ingenious, as harmonious, and as well-built as those boats. But the high seas beckon to him in vain, for his life is under an ill star. Modernism turns out to be his doom. The hero was not provided for in it; it has no use for this type.[13]

The doom of the modern poet is to desire to voyage out on the seas of poetic tradition, to traverse them and leave in his wake the record of a

[12]Walter Benjamin, *Charles Baudelaire*, trans. Harry Zohn (London: New Left Books, 1973), p. 74.

[13]Ibid., pp. 95-96. Further elucidation of the allegorical style of Baudelaire's lyrics, allegory producing the characteristic stylistic features in Baudelaire's poetry, occurs further on, pp. 98-100.

successful journey, only to suffer disastrous shipwreck, like the *Titanic* in Hardy's "The Convergence of the Twain," or the *Deutschland* in Hopkins's great ode. With Crispin in Stevens's "The Comedian as the Letter C," the modern poet inevitably becomes "an introspective voyager." He wanders, like Wordsworth's Newton, that figure for what Wordsworth recognized and most feared in himself—the solipsistic Imagination, "through strange seas of Thought alone" (1850 *Prelude*, III, 63). The modern yearning after the heroic turns into mere performance, the modern hero-poet is borne, Hamlet-like, to the stage to play the part that was written for him before his birth and will dominate his every gesture until death: "For the modern hero is no hero; he acts heroes. Heroic modernism turns out to be a tragedy in which the hero's part is available."[14]

For Hopkins, the preeminent hero was Christ, though lesser avatars appear in his poetry in such figures as Harry Ploughman, the laborer in "Tom's Garland," Felix Randal, the young boy in "The Bugler's First Communion," the shepherd in "The shepherd's brow, fronting forked lightening," and the soldier in the untitled poem about him written near the end of Hopkins's life. These figures populate Hopkins's poems and suggest the sad contrast between them and the poetic voice, the "lyrical I" which speaks of their courage, their strength, their transfiguration of suffering into triumph and joy. What fascinates and attracts Hopkins most in Christ and in the various laborers is how they make their strength manifest, how their triumph is produced in a showing forth of self which stands in stark and forbidding contrast to the poet's "wrecks and ruins." For Hopkins had always "that within which passes show," his poems "but the trappings and the suits of woe."

The epigraph to Hopkins's early poem, "Nondum,"—taken from Isaiah 45:15—is "Verily Thou art a God that hidest Thyself" (P, 32). It was Hopkins's fate to remain similarly hidden, his only reader another poet whose reception of Hopkins's work was at best equivocal. That Hopkins's *oeuvre* remained unpublished until long after his death, that he wrote in obscurity, virtually in secret, this fact of his poetic life cannot be overemphasized. Geoffrey Hartman has recently remarked a similar feature in Wordsworth's career:

> We should not forget that Wordsworth's greatest poem remained hidden, and that its power and authority (in the light of which we *now* read everything else) was but alluded to in the rest of his oeuvre. . . . Keeping *The Prelude* in reserve, almost like God his own Son,

[14]Ibid., p. 97.

Wordsworth reposed on a text-experience whose life remained with God.[15]

But the very notation of this similarity between the ostensible father-figure of modern English poetry and one of his more troubled (and troubling) heirs makes the essential difference between them immediately evident. For Wordsworth, keeping himself hidden was the condition of poetic strength; *The Prelude* provided an untapped reserve of poetic energy upon which to draw in his struggle against the fading of his "visionary gleam." Hopkins's hidden verse was less a comforting sign of achievement than a chastisement, a heavy burden from the past that weighed increasingly on his spirit as the years passed and no fresh burst of creative energy came. This is what makes Hopkins the more charac-teristically modern poet, for if Wordsworth exemplifies the modernist propensity to hesitate before the duty of speech (his verses "gain time by a characteristic *whiling*," Hartman shrewdly judges),[16] he nevertheless, in contrast to his descendants, keeps speech alive, and with it the possibility that the poetic fire, the visionary gleam, may yet one day revive. We know from the manuscripts of *The Prelude* that some of its finest lines were written in the last years of Wordsworth's life. Similar claims have been made for Yeats and for Hardy, but for how many countless others, the true moderns in this sense, have the creative energies of youth yielded little more than the promise of a brilliant future? For how many has Auden's melancholy judgment, "Poetry makes nothing happen," marked the daunting recognition that nothing can be done at all—that is, for poetry, nothing can be said at all? Though Harold Bloom may be correct to judge that "what is weak is forgettable and will be forgotten. Only strength is memorable,"[17] he knows very well (who better?) how para-doxical, how elusive, how rare is poetic strength. A careful reading of his recent work reveals that among modern English poets only Wordsworth achieved real strength, though at what cost to himself and to his reputation as poet in the last forty years of his life we know. I don't believe that we are yet in a position to dismiss as merely "weak" the poetry that has been written in the shadow of Wordsworth. This world, theirs and ours, is still too much with us.

In the pages that follow, I have attempted to position Hopkins within this melancholy fate of the moderns, within that shared consciousness of

---

[15]Geoffrey H. Hartman, "Words, Wish, Worth: Wordsworth," in Harold Bloom, et al., *Deconstruction and Criticism* (New York: Seabury Press, 1979), p. 213.

[16]Ibid., p. 204.

[17]Harold Bloom, "The Breaking of Form," in *Deconstruction and Criticism*, p. 5.

their own belatedness which Harold Bloom has studied with so much vigor and erudition. That we are only now beginning to discern the outlines of this situation in modern poetry, that criticism is just now trying to catch up with the conditions of its own time should come as no surprise, for criticism too suffers from the same historical disease as the poems it confronts. Standing in the long shadows of Dr. Johnson and Coleridge, contemporary criticism repeats their impassioned efforts to bring literature under the sway of rational categories, with no more success and a good deal more frustration ending in failure. For this too is modernism, the situation of "the poet in an age of prose," as Erich Heller has recently put it. This age, our age, has its exemplary ascetics before it: Hopkins, Mallarmé, Valéry. To take the measure of their achievement is to set the standard for our own. We write, they instruct us, only at our peril.

I   HOPKINS'S AESTHETICS

> Looking at a thing gradually merges into contemplation, contemplation into thinking, thinking is establishing connections, and thus it is possible to say that every attentive glance which we cast on the world is an act of theorizing.
>
> —*Goethe*

> In fact there is no theory that is not a fragment, carefully prepared, of some autobiography.
>
> —*Valéry*

GERARD MANLEY HOPKINS is remembered primarily for having written a handful of carefully crafted but obscure poems of exquisite beauty. His poetry has been variously considered as: in the line of a poetic tradition originating more or less with Keats, descending through Tennyson and Robert Bridges to Dylan Thomas, C. Day Lewis, and W. H. Auden; perhaps the most important voice among the group of poets who were part of or were significantly influenced by the pre-Raphaelite brotherhood, a group including Meredith, the Rosettis, and Swinburne; the vital link between the metaphysical poetry of the seventeenth century and the modernist poetry of Yeats, Eliot, and Pound; the most influential and important preserver of "what may be called the Shakespearian (as opposed to the Miltonic) potentialities of English."[1] He is also remembered as the coiner of a set of terms for describing his own poetic practice that have passed into general usage in discussions of poetry—inscape, instress, sprung rhythm, overthought, and underthought. But Hopkins was also a precise and rigorous theoretician of poetry, a poet-aesthetician not unlike his virtual contemporary Mallarmé and Mallarmé's most important disciple Valéry. Hopkins's theories of poetry and beauty command our attention for two reasons: first, they are basic to any understanding of his poetry; second, along with the aesthetic speculations of Coleridge, they are the most important nineteenth-century precursor in English of certain

---

[1] F. R. Leavis, "Metaphysical Isolation," in *Gerard Manley Hopkins by the Kenyon Critics* (Norfolk: New Directions, 1945), p. 134.

of the more important strains in contemporary poetics. As a theoretician, Hopkins anticipates many of the pronouncements of the Russian Formalists, some aspects of the work of English-speaking critics like William Empson and Kenneth Burke, and also some of the more recent deconstructive theories of Paul de Man, Harold Bloom, and J. Hillis Miller. Hopkins is, to borrow Ralph Freedman's epithet for Valéry, a "protean critic."[2]

Hopkins's writings on poetry and aesthetics evince a recurring tension, which is expressed by Hopkins himself as a contrasting of two kinds of beauty, chromatic and diatonic. These terms or their equivalent occur in several places in his early diaries (J, 76, 84, 104) and also, apropos of Hopkins's musical compositions, in a letter to Bridges written in 1883 (L. I, 182). The distinction between chromatic and diatonic beauty remained an important one for Hopkins, even though the actual terms do not recur often in his later writings. The opposition between the two terms is most fully explained in Hopkins's youthful imitation of a Platonic dialogue, "On the Origin of Beauty." Their meaning is explained by a character who is supposed to be a professor of aesthetics and whose opinions are certainly those of Hopkins himself. All beauty, the Professor contends, can be classed either as chromatic or diatonic, as "continuous" or "non-continuous," as transitional or separated by fixed intervals. Now poetry is characterized primarily by parallelism, which "is the cause of metaphor, simile, and antithesis," and parallelism is "put under the head of diatonic beauty" (J, 106). The Professor later elaborates: "Verse is distinguished from prose as employing a continuous structural parallelism, ranging from the technically so-called parallelism of the Psalms to the intricate structure of Greek or Italian or English verse" (J, 108). Poetry is distinguished by its artificial structure, by the organization of its parts into patterns formed by the intervals between elements. Like Wordsworth and Coleridge, Hopkins clearly distinguishes verse from prose and demands that poetic language be essentially different from ordinary language: "It is plain that metre, rhythm, rhyme, and all the structure which is called verse both necessitate and engender a difference in diction and in thought" (J, 84).

As Roman Jakobson, the Russian Formalists, and the American New Critics all claim, poetic language is qualitatively different from ordinary language. What distinguishes poetry from ordinary language, for Hopkins

---

[2]See Freedman's essay, "Paul Valéry," in *Modern French Criticism*, ed. John K. Simon (Chicago: University of Chicago Press, 1972), pp. 1-40.

as for Jakobson and the Formalists, is artifice or structure, what Hopkins calls parallelism:

> But what the character of poetry is will be found best by looking at the structure of verse. . . . The structure of poetry is that of continuous parallelism. . . . But parallelism is of two kinds necessarily — where the opposition is clearly marked, and where it is transitional rather or chromatic. Only the first kind, that of marked parallelism, is concerned with the structure of verse — in rhythm, the recurrence of a certain sequence of syllables, in metre, the recurrence of a certain sequence of rhythm, in alliteration, in assonance and in rhyme. Now the force of this recurrence is to beget a recurrence or parallelism answering to it in the words or thought and, speaking roughly and rather for the tendency than the invariable result, the more marked parallelism in structure whether of elaboration or of emphasis begets more marked parallelism in the words and sense. And moreover parallelism in expression tends to beget or passes into parallelism in thought. [J, 84-85]

This passage can be compared to a similar position taken by Jakobson: "In poetry not only the phonological sequence but in the same way any sequence of semantic units strives to build an equation. Similarity super-imposed on contiguity imparts to poetry its thoroughgoing symbolic, multiplex, polysemantic essence."[3] Poetry is a kind of language distinguished by structural regularities, not only in patterned sound sequences (rhyme, meter), but also on the semantic level. According to Jakobson and Hopkins, the phonological structure and the semantic structure influence and condition each other reciprocally.

It would be a mistake to construe this view as privileging phonological structure over semantic structure, making correspondences in meaning dependent upon prior sound correspondences. The semantic level of poetic language is not completely determined by the phonological level, nor are sound correspondences completely determined by semantic considerations. Hopkins and Jakobson subtly but significantly alter the intent of Pope's famous pronunciamento — the sound does not echo the sense so much as each reverberates against the other. It is as if an echo could originate in and by itself without an initial burst of sound to give rise to it. Similarly, it would be incorrect to say that poetry is simply an ornate

[3]Roman Jakobson, "Closing Statement," in *Style in Language*, ed. Thomas A. Sebeok (Cambridge: MIT Press, 1960), p. 370. Jakobson cites approvingly the passage from Hopkins just quoted. For Hopkins's later speculations on pattern or structure in poetry, see "Rhythm and Other Structural Parts of Rhetoric — Verse" (J, 267).

or highly rhetorical instance of ordinary language. As Jakobson points out, repeating the doctrine of the Moscow Linguistic Circle: "Poeticalness is not a supplementation of discourse with rhetorical adornment but a total re-evaluation of the discourse and of all its components whatso-ever."[4] Poetry is not merely the obedient and subservient offspring of ordinary language, but its Oedipal rival. Language is always already poetry.

According to Hopkins, poetry is distinguished by its "continuous and regular artificial structure" (J, 107). This structure is relational or, as Geoffrey Hartman has put it, diacritical.[5] As the professor of aesthetics remarks in "On the Origin of Beauty": "It seems then that it is not the excellence of any two things (or more) in themselves, but those two things as viewed by the light of each other, that makes beauty" (J, 93). As we have seen, Hopkins distinguishes two kinds of structural relations in art: chromatic and diatonic. Both types of structure are present in a work of art, but Hopkins favors diatonism over chromatism. Hopkins images this opposition in yet another way in some notes made several years after he wrote "On the Origin of Beauty." In these later notes, he distinguishes two kinds of mental activity demanded by the work of art, transition and contemplation:

> The mind has two kinds of energy, a transitional kind, when one thought or sensation follows another, which is to reason, whether actively as in deliberation, criticism, or passively, so to call it, as in reading etc; (ii) an abiding kind for which I remember no name, in which the mind is absorbed (as far as that may be), taken up by, dwells upon, enjoys, a single thought: we may call it contempla-tion. . . .
>
> Art exacts this energy of contemplation but also the other one, and in fact they are not incompatible, for even in the successive arts as music, for full enjoyment, the sythesis of the succession should give, unlock, the contemplative enjoyment of the unity of the whole. It is however true that in the successive arts with their greater complexity and length the whole's unity retires, is less important, serves rather for the framework of that of the parts. [J, 125-26]

The perception of diatonism through contemplation is inhibited by the property of successive arts (poetry and music) to engage the mind in

---

[4]Jakobson, "Closing Statement," p. 377.
[5]Geoffrey Hartman, "Hopkins Revisited," in *Beyond Formalism* (New Haven: Yale University Press, 1970), p. 239.

following transitional effects. The structure of a poem or of a quartet is to some extent invisible to the mind, though it can be discovered by dint of extreme attention and exertion. Paradoxically, the more the structure permeates the whole, the more difficult it is to apprehend:

> The further in anything, as a work of art, the organisation is carried out, the deeper the form penetrates, the prepossession flushes the matter, the more effort will be required in apprehension, the more power of comparison, the more capacity for receiving that synthesis of (either successive or spatially distinct) impressions which gives us the unity with the prepossession conveyed by it. [J, 126]

Hopkins mediates his earlier sharp distinction between chromatism and diatonism, for the more deeply embedded the diatonic structure in a work of art, the closer the intervals come to resemble chromatic transitions. In short, the more highly and intricately structured a work is, the more it will appear to have no structure or organization at all. The danger in this tendency toward structured complexity is that it seduces the mind into unraveling successive impressions without being able to integrate them into an ordered whole:

> The saner moreover is the act of contemplation as contemplating that which really is expressed in the object.
>   But some minds prefer that the prepossession they are to receive should be conveyed by the least organic, expressive, by the most suggestive, way. By this means the prepossession and the definition, uttering, are distinguished and unwound, which is the less sane attitude. [J, 126]

Small wonder that Hopkins remarks that "contemplation in its absoluteness is impossible unless in a trance" (J, 126).

In these notes, Hopkins develops a theory of form, perhaps the fundamental category of all aesthetic speculation, and one of the central motifs in Western philosophy since Plato. But Hopkins's theory of form is not identical with, though it is necessarily a party to, that logocentric or idealist tradition of which Plato is the most celebrated exemplar. For Hopkins, form is eccentric, realist, differential. Like Stevens, he knows "the eccentric to be the base of design."[6] His is a theory of decentered form, similar to contemporary deconstructive theories of interpretation, which are admittedly not at all new in the Western tradition.

---

[6]Wallace Stevens, "Like Decorations in a Nigger Cemetery," in *The Collected Poems of Wallace Stevens* (New York: Alfred A. Knopf, 1954), p. 151.

To cite one example in Hopkins's own era, consider the following passage from George Eliot's essay, "Notes on Form in Art" (1868):

> Fundamentally, form is unlikeness, as is seen in the philosophic use of the word Form in distinction from Matter; & in consistency with this fundamental meaning, every difference is form. Thus, sweetness is a form of sensibility, rage is a form of passion, green is a form both of light & of sensibility. . . . And as knowledge continues to grow by its alternating processes of distinction & combination, seeing smaller & smaller unlikenesses & grouping or associating these under a common likeness, it arrives at the conception of wholes composed of parts more & more multiplied & highly differenced, yet more & more absolutely bound together by various conditions of common likeness or mutual dependence. And the fullest example of such a whole is the highest example of Form: in other words, the relation of multiplex interdependent parts to a whole which is itself in the most varied & therefore the fullest relation to other wholes. . . . The highest Form, then, is the highest organism, that is to say, the most varied group of relations bound together in a wholeness which again has the most varied relations with all other phenomena.[7]

Form does not originate in the imposition of a structure on a series of diverse elements, but in the spontaneous generation of similarity out of difference. As Gilles Deleuze puts it, "seul ce qui se ressemble diffère, seules les différences se ressemblent."[8] Form does not radiate from a center but arises spontaneously from the comparison and differentiation of separate and distinctive parts within the whole. George Eliot elaborates this idea with respect to form in poetry:

> Poetic Form was not begotten by thinking it out or framing it as a shell which should hold emotional expression, any more than the shell of an animal arises before the living creature; but emotion, by its tendency to repetition, i.e. rhythmic persistence in proportion as diversifying thought is absent, creates a form by the recurrence of its elements in adjustment with certain given conditions of sound, language, action, or environment. Just as the beautiful expanding curves of a bivalve shell are not first made for the reception of the

[7]George Eliot, "Notes on Form in Art," in *Essays of George Eliot*, ed. Thomas Pinney (New York: Columbia University Press, 1963), pp. 432-33.
[8]Gilles Deleuze, *Logique du sens* (Paris: Editions de Minuit, 1969), p. 302.

unstable inhabitant, but grow & are limited by the simple rhythmic conditions of its growing life.[9]

Poetic form is produced by the recurrence of difference. Chromatism and diatonism are not mutually exclusive but mutually constitutive. The differential structure of diatonism depends upon the successive repetitions of chromatism, and chromatic succession includes diatonic intervals in its differentiation. The dialectic of resemblance and difference generates the unity of differentiated parts that is the poem.

Hopkins himself examines the concept of form in art in a manner similar to George Eliot in a passage on rhythmical variation in poetry. Differences in rhythmic structure do not shatter the unity of a work; on the contrary, only such differences can give the work explicit formal coherence:

It should be understood that these various means of breaking the sameness of rhythm and especially caesura do not break the unity of the verse but the contrary; they make it organic and what is organic is one. All the parts of water are alike but the parts of a man's body differ and man's individuality is marked but the individual being a waterdrop has is gone when it falls into water again. And in everything the more remote the ratio of the parts to one another or the whole the greater the unity if felt at all, as in the circle and ellipse, for the circle is felt to be more at one and one thing than the ellipse, yet the ratio of its circumference to its diameter is undiscoverable, whereas there must be one ellipse in which it is 3:1 and any number

[9]George Eliot, Essays, p. 435. The analogy between poetic form and the organic form of the shell of a mollusk is immensely suggestive, particularly in light of the essay by Paul Valéry, "Man and the Sea Shell." Valéry echoes George Eliot's comments on the rhythmic regularity of the sea shell's form and elaborates this idea via the analogy of music: "In this invincible and one might say flawless progression of form, which involves and develops its whole setting according to the continuous fatality of its convolutions and seems to create its own time, we admire the combination of *rhythm*, marked by the regular spots or spines, and of *indivisible movement*. It is like seeing music. The correspondence of ornaments on successive spirals suggests a counterpoint, while the continuity sustains the main theme of the rotation of the surface" (Paul Valéry, "Man and the Sea Shell," in Aesthetics, trans. Ralph Manheim [New York: Pantheon Books, 1964], p. 6). For Valéry, the sea shell is the emblem of all formal beauty. The form of the shell is derived from a basic dissymmetry between the forward movement of the developing shell and the ornamental figures (spots and spines) that interpose themselves within this movement. Valéry claims that this principle of dissymmetry (which recalls George Eliot's "Fundamentally, form is unlikeness") is an irreducible aspect of the mind's relations to nature, hence, the constitutive element in all perception of formal beauty. On the irreducible distinction in Romantic aesthetics between mind and nature, see Michael Sprinker, "Ruskin on the Imagination," Studies in Romanticism 18 (Spring 1979): 115-39.

of others in which it is any ratio we like to take between π and 2. [J, 283][10]

This is a confusing passage, and it would seem to contradict what I have said about Hopkins's notion of form as decentered or eccentric. Hopkins's image for perfect formal unity is the circle, which suggests complete homogeneity and an undifferentiated relationship of part to whole, all points in the circumference of the circle being equidistant from the center. But Hopkins is more concerned here with the ratio of diameter to circumference, which he says is "undiscoverable." Presumably, he means that the precise ratio cannot be determined, that π is a figure whose exact magnitude is unknown. The form of a circle is perfectly unified; the relation of the parts to the whole is apparent (one perceives the figure of a circle and recognizes its formal structure) and yet at the same time mysterious (the precise ratio of the parts to the whole is indeterminate). Similarly, in poetry the more highly differentiated and thus varied the rhythm (Hopkins mentions caesura, tonic accent, emphatic accent, breaking of vowel sound, alliteration, and rhyme as means of varying the rhythm), the greater the potential for formal unity. As Hopkins once wrote to Bridges apropos of the metrical pattern of "The Wreck of the Deutschland": "There is no conceivable licence I shd. not be able to justify, that with all my licences, or rather laws, I am stricter than you and I might say than anybody I know. . . . So that I may say my apparent licences are counterbalanced, and more, by my strictness" (L. I, 44-45).

Sprung rhythm metrically objectifies Hopkins's theory of form, and "The Wreck of the Deutschland" is, according to this standard of judgment, his most formally perfect poem. Hopkins always contended that he

[10] The notion that formal unity is an organic quality is also central to the passage quoted from George Eliot's "Notes on Form in Art." Like Hopkins, George Eliot finds an analogy for aesthetic form in the human body (see "Notes," in *Essays*, p. 433). The emergence of the organic model of aesthetic form in the eighteenth and nineteenth centuries is discussed by M. H. Abrams in *The Mirror and the Lamp* (New York: Oxford University Press, 1953), pp. 156-225. The subsequent history of organic form in modernist literature is too vast a subject to discuss here. A single example, suggestive of the continuity between Romanticism and modernism, will serve. According to Stuart Gilbert, Joyce's schema for the structuring of *Ulysses* included a parallel between organs of the body and the episode of the *Odyssey* to which the narrative corresponded. Gilbert argues that for Joyce the novel was, on one level, formally analogous to the structure of the human body. Moreover, Gilbert's own description (endorsed and in part suggested by Joyce himself) of the novel's structural principles is termed "The Rhythm of *Ulysses*" and refers back to the description of the aesthetic principle of rhythm given by Stephen Dedalus in *A Portrait of the Artist as a Young Man* (see Stuart Gilbert, *James Joyce's Ulysses*, 2nd ed. rev. [New York: Alfred A. Knopf, 1952], pp. 36-43. Organicism, rhythm, elaboration of form through differential repetition—these are the aesthetic principles that connect *Ulysses* to "The Wreck of the Deutschland."

did not invent sprung rhythm but merely discovered it in previous poetry and exploited its resources in his own. In the preface he wrote for his poems, he explained that sprung rhythm extends the principle of counterpoint found in Milton's *Samson Agonistes*, where two rhythms seem to be mounted one on top of the other. But moving one step further, counterpoint yields to sprung rhythm properly speaking: "And in fact if you counterpoint throughout, since one only of the counter rhythms is actually heard, the other is really destroyed or cannot come to exist and what is written is one rhythm only and probably Sprung Rhythm" (P, 47).[11] Sprung rhythm would appear, then, to have no princple of regularity governing the stresses. In theory, any word can be emphasized, and any number of words in a given line can bear primary stress. But as Hopkins actually employs sprung rhythm in "The Wreck of the Deutschland," the metrical structure is in fact quite regular. Each stanza of the poem is carefully spaced to indicate the number of stresses in each line, and, with the exception of the first ten stanzas, which have only two stresses in the opening line, the distribution of stresses in every stanza is the same: 3-3-4-3-5-5-4-6. What appears to be a chaos of different rhythms turns out to be a pattern of intricately arranged stresses. Though Hopkins's metrics seem to be "licentious," they are in fact as strictly regular as the stanzas of the *Faerie Queene*. This is the very essence of Hopkins's achievement of form. Counterpointed rhythm varies the regularity of meter to produce difference against the background of form; sprung rhythm produces form out of original difference.

Harold Whitehall's otherwise excellent essay on sprung rhythm errs in this respect, that he believes sprung rhythm to be a variation of the natural regularity of all rhythm: "Consciously or subconsciously, [Hopkins] had come to realize that a metrical foot represents a unit in a series of even-time (isochronous) units and that, if these even-time units are in some manner marked off for the perception of the reader, their time-lapses may be occupied by anything from a single heavily stressed syllable to four or five syllables. In short, granted a rhythmic regularity based upon even-time units, stress arrangements within the individual units can be varied almost at will."[12] This is an excellent description of counter-

[11] The origin of sprung rhythm and the principles it enacts are also discussed by Hopkins in a letter to Canon Dixon dated October 5, 1878 (L. II, 14-15). I discuss this letter and sprung rhythm in greater detail in chapter 4.

[12] Harold Whitehall, "Sprung Rhythm," in *Gerard Manley Hopkins by the Kenyon Critics*, p. 36. Whitehall's contention that sprung rhythm is based upon the natural even-time units in all metrical feet is criticized by Father Ong in his classic study of Hopkins's metrical practice, "Hopkins' Sprung Rhythm and the Life of English Poetry," in *Immortal Diamond*, ed. Norman Weyand, S.J. (New York: Sheed & Ward, 1949), pp. 145-47.

point, but it distorts the fundamental characteristic of sprung rhythm—its complete independence from any original or natural pattern of stress. Sprung rhythm does not emerge from an originally regular pattern of stress, but the other way around. Rhythm is produced for Hopkins by the recurrence of stresses in a differentiated but originally formless mass of stressed and unstressed syllables. As Hopkins once wrote to Bridges: "I look on rhythm as a rule, not as a law; as a convention, not as a nature" (L. I, 261).

It is clear from reading the notes entitled "Rhythm and the Other Structural Parts of Rhetoric—Verse" (J, 267-90) that Hopkins considered rhythm among the most crucial problems in poetics, partly because of his intuition that "once music and verse were one" (J, 268), but above all because of his conviction that "verse is speech having a marked figure, order / of sounds independent of meaning" (J, 267). The shape of verse, its formal structure, is primarily determined by its rhythm. But rhythm itself is not a univocal concept. It is produced by a kind of tensional play between stress and pitch. This play is evident in all languages and may be said to be one of the characteristics differentiating one language from another:

> We may think of words as heavy bodies, as indoor or out of door objects of nature or man's art. Now every visible palpable body has a centre of gravity round which it is in balance and a centre of illumination or *highspot* or *quickspot* up to which it is lighted and down from which it is shaded. The centre of gravity is like the accent of stress, the highspot like the accent of pitch, for pitch is like light and colour, stress like weight, and as in some things as air and water the centre of gravity is either unnoticeable or changeable so there may be languages in a fluid state in which there is little difference of weight or stress between syllables or what there is changes and again as it is only glazed bodies that shew the highspot well so there may be languages in which the pitch is unnoticeable. [J, 269]

English is a language without noticeable pitch; French is a language in which pitch is more marked and stress relatively weak. The difference between pitch and stress reflects the distinction between chromatism and diatonism. Pitch changes subtly, by minute gradations or transitions, as in the chromatic scale with its half-tones. Stress corresponds to diatonic intervals, which are emphatically marked, just as stressed syllables are sharply differentiated from unstressed ones. But all words can be pitched and stressed at once, as all bodies with mass are both illuminated and weighted. Words possess this double quality or principle of complementarity between pitch and stress which verse produces in rhythmic patterns.[13] For Hopkins, verse is both weighted (stressed) and colored (pitched); rhythm is the ordered play produced by the difference between these two qualities.

But "pitch" and "stress" denote more than just musical qualities in Hopkins's writings. Elsewhere he employs the words to characterize the individuality of the self. For Hopkins, pitch is the essential quality of human individuality, the clarity of selfhood that separates man from the rest of creation: "I find myself both as man and as myself something most determined and distinctive, at pitch, more distinctive and higher pitched than anything else I see" (S, 122). Pitch is the distinctive and distinguishing feature of self: "Nothing else in nature comes near this unspeakable stress of pitch, distinctiveness, and selving, this self-being of my own" (S, 123). This "unspeakable stress of pitch" gives the self its sense of being, its difference from all other selves, from all other things in the world. But pitch is, in a sense, something given, a primordial quality of the self. It can be altered or intensified by the related but somewhat different characteristic of the self's being in the world—stress. Hopkins explains stress in a striking passage on the suffering of the lost souls in Hell who experience the pain of fire and brimstone. The meaning of this pain is something more than purely physical sensation:

> Our action leaves in our minds scapes or species, the extreme "intention" or instressing of which would be painful and the pain would be that of fire, supposing fire to be the condition of a body (and by analogy of any substance) *texturally at stress*. The soul then can be instressed *in* the species or scape of any bodily action (whether this gives rise to a physical and quantitative extension of its substance or not) and so *towards* the species or scape of any object, as of sight, sound, taste, smell; and a high degree of such instress would in each case be the pain of fire, so that every other pain would be besides a pain of fire. [S, 136-37]

Just as stresses in a poetic line bring out the distinctive qualities of sound and meaning in language, so a body "texturally at stress" brings out the potential of the soul to experience suffering. All selves are pitched, possessing a tonal quality specific to themselves, but pitch is subject to

[13]Just as Whitehead found an analogous conceptualization to the space-time of modern physics in the poetry of Wordsworth and Shelley, I wish to draw an analogy between Bohr's principle of complementarity in quantum mechanics and Hopkins's conception of rhythm as the differential play between stress and pitch. The concept might also be compared to Derrida's "freeplay" in his essay, "Structure, Sign and Play in the Discourse of the Human Sciences," in *Writing and Difference*, trans. Alan Bass (Chicago: University of Chicago Press, 1978), pp. 278-93.

varying degrees of emphasis or stress. Hopkins employs the language of
his poetics (which he has derived from musicology) to express a theory of
the self, and it may be said in turn that the theory of the self is an expression of Hopkins's poetics. This is not simply a fortuitous correspondence
for Hopkins. Writing poetry was for him an act of enormous spritiual
significance, a primary expression of the will. It is not surprising, therefore,
that he chose a vocabulary drawn from poetics to describe the action of
the self in the world. Hopkins is the "more severe, / More harassing
master" of whom Wallace Stevens speaks in "An Ordinary Evening in
New Haven," for Hopkins's writings realize what Stevens himself desires
to produce in his poem. They "extemporize / Subtler, more urgent proof
that the theory / Of poetry is the theory of life, / As it is, in the intricate
evasions of as / In things seen and unseen, created from nothingness, /
The heavens, the hells, the worlds, the longed-for lands."[14] Hopkins's
career as a writer is powerful testimony to the inseparability of poetry
from life, of theory from poetry, of the self from the texts that it produces.
Thus perceived, Hopkins's writings find their true kinship in a body of
poetry and theory with whose immense influence contemporary poetry
and criticism have only just begun to cope. I mean the work of the French
Symbolists.

Had "The Wreck of the Deutschland" first been published in 1876,
rather than in 1918, it surely would have caused an even greater stir than
it did. To a Victorian whose taste was formed by the poetry of Tennyson,
Browning, and Arnold, Hopkins's verses would have seemed strange, out
of place, certainly not typical of nineteenth-century style. Small wonder
that he has been claimed as a peculiarly modern voice in English poetry
and that his poetic idiom has most often been compared to that of Yeats
and Dylan Thomas, rather than to that of his contemporaries. But
Hopkins's modernity is not limited to the rhythmic and phonological
aspects of his verse, nor can a just estimate of his achievement be made
simply by examining his relationship to English poetry. As a poet and an
aesthetician, Hopkins has numerous affinities with the most important
aesthetic movement of the second half of the nineteenth century, French
Symbolism. Just as the "true master" for Pound's Mauberley "was
Flaubert," so Hopkins's filiation to nineteenth-century aesthetics is most
apparent in the writings of Mallarmé and Valéry.

Hopkins can be linked to Mallarmé in a variety of ways, all more or
less indirect. Neither knew the work of the other, though the arcs of their
respective careers intersect at several junctures. Perhaps most obvious is

[14] Wallace Stevens, "An Ordinary Evening in New Haven," in *Collected Poems*, p. 486.

the "etymological" and "mythological" link. In 1878, Mallarmé published a curious work which was the fruit of some fourteen years of study of the English language, *Les Mots anglais*. On the title page, the work is identified as a "petite philologie," and it does indeed give an historical account of the development of English, emphasizing the two principal elements blended in modern English, French and Anglo-Saxon. As a piece of scholarship, the work is not particularly noteworthy, but it is important to recognize the similarity of interest in philological studies between Mallarmé and Hopkins, whose etymological speculations in his journals and diaries are a crucial aspect of his writing.[15] The great enthusiasm for philological studies that swept through England in the middle of the nineteenth century significantly affected the work of both poets. It would not be an exaggeration to say that Mallarmé's endless meditations on the nature of language and Hopkins's investigations of etymologies and the origin of language grow out of a common source, the efflorescence of historical language study, particularly in England, during the middle decades of the nineteenth century. In addition, for Hopkins, as for numerous nineteenth-century philologists, the study of language provided the key to many other human phenomena, including the vast and complicated field of comparative mythology. It can hardly be coincidental, then, that in 1880 Mallarmé also published a manual of comparative mythology, *Les Dieux antiques*, which was modeled on an earlier collection by George Cox. Mallarmé professed to have published both this work and *Les Mots anglais* for financial reasons, but it is also clear that these topics engaged his imagination quite as much as they fascinated and exercised Hopkins.[16] Both poets sought some fundamental or original

[15]Jacob Korg has noticed the resemblance between *Les Mots anglais* and Hopkins's etymological notes, pointing to the fact that some of the same etymologies appear in both texts. But Korg errs when he says that Mallarmé "goes further than Hopkins (attributing innate significance to the shape of letters, as well as to the sound) and considers each word a structure whose initial sound establishes a center of meaning that is modified by the subsequent sounds" (Jacob Korg, "Hopkins's Linguistic Deviations," *PMLA* 92 [October 1977]: 979). As I show in the next chapter in some of the citations from his etymological notes, Hopkins sometimes did attribute "innate significance" to certain sounds, deriving this notion from the imitative theory of the origin of language. Moreover, the sound changes in poems like "That Nature is a Heraclitean Fire" go very far toward the Mallarmean notion which "considers each word a structure whose initial sound establishes a center of meaning that is modified by the subsequent sounds." Korg wishes in the end to salvage a representational theory of language in Hopkins, an interpretation which my own reading of Hopkins strongly resists and which Hopkins himself (though with more ambivalence than I) resisted as well.

[16]Mallarmé wrote to Verlaine in 1885, in a letter that has come to be known as Mallarmé's "Autobiography": "J'ai dû faire, dans des moments de gêne ou pour acheter de ruineux

basis on which to construct their poetics, and in the nineteenth century such a basis seemed to many thinkers to be located in the historical study of language and the myths of ancient cultures.[17] Hopkins and Mallarmé are united by a shared longing for an original language that would universalize their poetic productions. For both writers, the creation of poetry was a metaphysical enterprise of great moment.

It was the nearly pathological seriousness with which they took the poet's task that led Mallarmé and Hopkins to similar spiritual crises in writing verse. Hopkins's feelings of sterility and impotence late in life, his inability to write or to produce work, are matched by Mallarmé's confessions of sterility and his despair of ever writing poetry. As early as 1862, he wrote to Henri Cazalis about "the strange feeling of sterility I have had this spring. After three futile months, I have finally gotten rid of it, and my first sonnet is meant to describe it—that is, to curse it."[18] More than two years later (at the age of twenty-two!), still plagued by a consciousness of futility and failure, Mallarmé believed his poetic career to be over: "I

---

canots, des besognes propres, et voilà tout (Dieux Antiques, Mots Anglais) dont il sied de ne pas parler" (Stéphane Mallarmé, *Oeuvres Complètes*, texte établi et annoté par Henri Mondor et G. Jean-Aubry [Paris: Bibliothèque de la Pléiade, 1945], p. 663).

[17]An important connection between Hopkins and Mallarmé existed in the person of Gaston Maspéro, the eminent Egyptologist, whose *Histoire des peuples d'Orient* Hopkins read with great care and interest (see L. III, 257-58, 259, 263, 264, 267). Maspéro was a friend of Mallarmé and a frequenter of the famous discussions that the latter held in his apartment in the rue de Rome (see Charles Mauron, *Introduction to the Psychoanalysis of Mallarmé*, trans. Archibald Henderson, Jr. and Will L. McLendon [Berkeley and Los Angeles: University of California Press, 1963], p. 29; and Henri Mondor, *Vie de Mallarmé* [Paris: Gallimard, 1941], pp. 367, 465). The seminal importance of philological and mythological studies of the intellectual phenomenon we call Romanticism cannot be doubted. The shape of the intellectual history of the last two centuries was powerfully affected by the discovery, translation, dissemination, and assimilation of oriental texts; nowhere was this influence more pronounced than in the poetry and prose of Romantic writers. Hugo, Flaubert, Renan, Herder, Schelling, Friedrich Schlegel, Coleridge, Ruskin, Byron, Shelley, and Pater —these and many other major figures in the history of Romanticism were decisively influenced by the body of texts and doctrine which Raymond Schwab (following Edgar Quinet) has called the "oriental Renaissance." On this topic, see: Raymond Schwab, *La Renaissance orientale* (Paris: Payot, 1950); Edward W. Said, *Orientalism* (New York: Pantheon, 1978); Hans Aarsleff, *The Study of Language in England, 1780-1860* (Princeton: Princeton University Press, 1967); and Michel Foucault, *The Order of Things*, a translation of *Les Mots et les choses* (New York: Random House, 1970). The most thorough examination of Hopkins's debt to Victorian philology can be found in James Milroy's *The Language of Gerard Manley Hopkins* (London: André Deutsch, 1977), pp. 39-69. On the foundation of Mallarmé's poetics in "the autonomy of the word" (an idea which developed out of comparative philology), see Jean-Pierre Richard, *L'Univers imaginaire de Mallarmé* (Paris: Université de Paris, Faculté des Lettres, 1961), pp. 528-36.

[18]Stéphane Mallarmé, *Selected Prose Poems, Essays and Letters*, trans. Bradford Cook (Baltimore: Johns Hopkins University Press, 1956), p. 81.

think that as far as poetry goes, I'm done: there are vast empty spaces in my mind; I am incapable of any consistent, close thought. And so, with this all too real, all too cruel degradation of my mind . . . , I am atoning for the excesses of my youth. I look upon myself with fear, as on a ruin. In all my letters I am going to lie to my friends and tell them I am working; but it won't be true. A poet on this earth should be purely a poet; whereas I, too often, am a corpse. I may some day deserve to be considered as an amateur, but no more than that."[19] Six months later, he had been writing and continued to do so, but always in the shadow of impending cessation: "I have left *Hérodiade* to cruel winter. I was sterilized by that lonely work."[20]

This crisis in Mallarmé's life continued for another four years, and though he emerged from it, he believed, strengthened and infused with an ideal of poetic beauty, he continued to be intimidated and haunted by the very ideal he had discovered. His confession of this ideal and his sad awareness that he could never realize it completely are fully elaborated in the "Autobiography":

> J'ai toujours rêvé et tenté autre chose, avec une patience d'alchimiste, prêt à y sacrifier toute vanité et toute satisfaction, comme on brûlait jadis son mobilier et les poutres de son toit, pour alimenter le fourneau du Grand Oeuvre. Quoi? c'est difficile à dire: un livre, tout bonnement, en maints tomes, un livre qui soit un livre, architectural et prémédité, et non un recueil des inspirations de hasard fussent-elles merveilleuses. . . . J'irai plus loin, je dirai: le Livre persuadé qu'au fond il n'y en a qu'un, tenté à son insu par quiconque a écrit, meme les Génies. L'explication orphique de la Terre, qui est le seul devoir du poëte et le jeu littéraire par excellence: car le rythme même du livre, alors impersonnel et vivant, jusque dans sa pagination, se juxtapose aux équations de ce rêve, ou Ode.
>
> Voilà l'aveu de mon vice, mis à nu, cher ami, que mille fois j'ai rejeté, l'esprit meurtri ou las, mais cela me possède et je réussirai peut-être; non pas à faire cet ouvrage dans son ensemble (il faudrait être je ne sais qui pour cela!) mais à en montrer un fragment d'exécuté.[21]

It would not be unjust to characterize Mallarmé's writing career as the continual production of fragments, a series of notes toward the "Grand Oeuvre" which he had discovered. Not even when taken together can his

[19]Ibid., p. 83.
[20]Ibid., pp. 85-86.
[21]Mallarmé, *Oeuvres Complètes*, pp. 662-63.

entire corpus be said to have achieved this lofty eminence. At the end of his life, he was working on his *Livre*, but left it unfinished, a chaotic mass of obscure musings.[22] And of the works he completed before his death, perhaps only *Un Coup de dés* can be said to have approached his goal of producing, "le livre, instrument spirituel."

Mallarmé's severe poetic ideal isolated him from reality, not merely from society, but from the real world itself. A fitting epigraph for his writing would be the phrase from *Igitur:* "moi projeté absolu."[23] As Georges Poulet has argued, this isolation of the self from reality is the essence of Mallarmé's poetic:

> Mallarmean poetry constitutes itself in a closed circuit. It is the double reflection which, across the void, through the window glass, the two halves of a thought that tries to think itself, exchange. . . . It attempts to exist solely in a relationship of exchange from the self to the self, in a purely interior movement in which the given and the rendered back are equivalent; in a perpetual movement.[24]

Mallarmé's poems strive for what Karlheinz Stierle has called "auto-referentiality,"[25] or what Poulet labels "atony."[26] Poulet's word is a good one, since the model of musical composition is intimately connected to the Mallarmean ideal of poetry. Mallarmé's writings provide abundant evidence that music presented to him a perfect image for the goal of poetic form. In "Le livre, instrument spirituel," he boldly proclaims: "La Poésie, proche l'idée, est Musique, par excellence—ne consent pas d'infériorité." The formal arrangements of poetry must liberate "l'air ou chant sous le texte." The identity of musical and poetic form distinguishes poetry from "mere talking": "L'écrit, envol tacite d'abstraction, reprend ses droits en face de la chute des sons nus: tous deux, Musique et lui, intimant une préalable disjonction, celle de la parole, certainement par

[22]For a description of Mallarmé's *Livre*, see Mauron, *Introduction to the Psychoanalysis of Mallarmé*, pp. 238-41. On the *Livre* as the culmination of all the Mallarmean themes and the final goal of all his writing, see Richard, *L'Univers imaginaire de Mallarmé*, pp. 565-74.

[23]Mallarmé, *Oeuvres Complètes*, p. 434.

[24]Georges Poulet, *The Interior Distance*, trans. Elliott Coleman (1959; rpt. Ann Arbor: University of Michigan Press, 1964), p. 238.

[25]Karlheinz Stierle, "Position and Negation in Mallarmé's 'Prose pour Des Esseintes,'" trans. Sibylle Kisro, *Yale French Studies* 54 (1977): 96-117. On the limitations of the concept of auto-referentiality for interpreting lyric poetry, with specific reference to Stierle's interpretations of Mallarmé, see Paul de Man, "Lyric and Modernity," in *Blindness and Insight* (New York: Oxford University Press, 1971), pp. 166-86.

[26]Poulet, *Interior Distance*, p. 252 et passim.

effroi de fournir au bavardage."[27] As in a musical composition, the relation of one element to another constitutes the structure of the poem:

> No successful poem can be written by Chance: that is the central fact which several of us have discovered and proved. I think that once we have perfectly defined poetic form, our principal aim should be to make the words of a poem self-mirroring (since they are sufficiently autonomous to begin with and need no outside impression) to such an extent that no one of them will seem to have a color of its own, and all of them will be merely the notes of a scale.[28]

As Poulet admirably characterizes "the Mallarmean poem," it resembles "a musical accompaniment which at the same time conceals and reinforces the principal theme."[29]

Of course Mallarmé was scarcely alone among nineteenth-century writers in attributing ideal aesthetic form to music. Schopenhauer, Nietzsche, Proust, and Pater come immediately to mind as equally important disciples of this aesthetic creed.[30] But it is in the work of Mallarmé's friend and poetic heir, Paul Valéry, that the relationship of musical to poetic form is most lucidly and completely adumbrated. Valéry was twenty when he met Mallarmé for the first time in 1891. Along with Leonardo and Poe, Mallarmé was among the earliest and most lasting influences on Valéry's thought, particularly on his aesthetics. Valéry saw in Mallarmé a turning point in the history of poetic art, a figure who

---

[27] Mallarmé, *Oeuvres Complètes*, pp. 381, 387, 385.

[28] Mallarmé, *Selected Prose Poems, Essays and Letters*, p. 93.

[29] Poulet, *Interior Distance*, p. 276. In a later essay on Mallarmé's "Prose pour Des Esseintes," Poulet suggests that this prose poem is modeled on ecclesiastical hymns, which Mallarmé "closely imitates" but subverts at the same time (Poulet, *The Metamorphoses of the Circle*, trans. Carley Dawson and Elliott Coleman [Baltimore: Johns Hopkins University Press, 1966], p. 291).

[30] The central figure around whom so many members of this constellation were arranged was Richard Wagner, whose operas were among the most influential works of art produced during the nineteenth century, especially in France and Germany. Mallarmé wrote a famous essay on Wagner (before he had ever heard a note of his music performed!), and Proust devoted numerous pages of *À la recherche du temps perdu* to meditations on the formal beauty of Wagner's music. The peculiar spell that the ideal of musical form has cast over modern aesthetics is one of the principal themes in the work of Erich Heller. See especially his essays, "The Realistic Fallacy" and "The Artist's Journey into the Interior," in *The Artist's Journey into the Interior and Other Essays* (New York: Random House, 1965). Heller sees in the celebration of music as an aesthetic (and ethical) ideal the outcome of a general tendency of the European mind toward inwardness·which is visible in poetry, philosophy, and the visual arts since the Renaissance. For Heller, the apotheosis of this inner dialectic in European art and thought (which he calls, following Hegel, "Romanticism") is Rilke's "Gesang ist Dasein."

stood for the salvation of poetry in the modern world. To save poetry, Mallarmé brought it closer to music:

> The problem of Mallarmé's whole life, the perpetual object of his meditations, of his subtlest researches, was, as we know, how to win back for poetry the empire that had been seized by the great modern composers. . . . Beset and irritated, as it were, by the problem of power, Mallarmé had approached literature as no one before him had ever done: with a depth, a rigorous logic, a sort of instinct for deducing laws that made him akin—without the great poet's ever suspecting it— to some of those modern geometricians who transformed the basis of the science, giving it a new scope and power by a closer and closer analysis of its fundamental notions and necessary conventions.[31]

What Mallarmé produced in poetry was a "text" with "no solution; that is, no equivalent in prose. It has no *subject* distinct from itself, but a sort of *program* consisting of a collection of words, among which certain *conjunctions as important as nouns* and types of *syntactical moments* (that is, components of forms) and above all, a table of the tonalities of words, etc." Mallarmé's ideal was "absolute poetry," a poetry that would attain the formal unity and the independence from sentiment of a Bach fugue, a poetry "whose entire beauty consists in its combinations, in the construction of a separate intuitive order."[32]

The powerful and inspiring example of Mallarmé continued to dominate Valéry's aesthetic thought and poetic practice throughout his career. Writing about the difference between the "universe" of poetry and the "universe" of the real world, Valéry announces: "But poetry requires or suggests a very different 'Universe': a universe of reciprocal relations analogous to the universe of sounds within which musical thought is born and moves. In this poetic universe, resonance triumphs over

---

[31] Paul Valéry, "The Existence of Symbolism," in *Leonardo, Poe, Mallarmé*, trans. Malcolm Cowley and James R. Lawler (Princeton: Princeton University Press, 1972), pp. 231-32.

[32] Valéry, *Leonardo, Poe, Mallarmé*, pp. 395, 266. Cf. the following passage from Wallace Stevens, written in explanation of section 7 of "The Man with the Blue Guitar": "I do not desire to exist apart from our works and the imagination does not desire to exist apart from our works. While this has a *double entendre*, still its real form is on the page. . . . A poem of symbols exists for itself" (*Letters of Wallace Stevens*, ed. Holly Stevens [New York: Alfred A. Knopf, 1966], p. 362). In a letter written the following day (August 10, 1940), Stevens identifies the goal of all poetry as "pure poetry" (pp. 363-64). Though Stevens later denied the influence of Mallarmé on his poetry (see the letter to Bernard Heringman dated May 3, 1949, in *Letters*, pp. 635-36), the ideal of "pure poetry" allies him with the aesthetics of Valéry, Mallarmé, and the Symbolists.

causality, and 'form,' far from dissolving into its effects, is as it were *recalled* by them. The Idea claims its voice."[33] This is an almost exact paraphrase of the Mallarmean goal to make "the words of a poem self-mirroring." As Valéry elsewhere suggests, words in poetry "act on us like a chord of music. The impression produced depends largely on resonance, rhythm, and the number of syllables."[34] In Valéry's poetics, not meanings but sounds and rhythms are the primary and original constituents of poetry:

> I should like to tell you a true story, so that you may feel as I felt, and in a curiously clear way, the whole difference that exists between the poetic state or emotion, even creative and original, and the production of a work. . . .
>
> I had left my house to relax from some tedious piece of work by walking and by a consequent change of scene. As I went along the street where I live, I was suddenly *gripped* by a rhythm which took possession of me and soon gave me the impression of some force outside myself. It was as though someone else were making use of my *living-machine*. Then another rhythm overtook and combined with the first, and certain strange *transverse* relations were set up between these two principles. . . . They combined the movement of my walking legs and some kind of song I was murmuring, or rather which was being murmured *through me*. This composition became more and more complicated and soon in its complexity went far beyond anything I could reasonably produce with my ordinary, usable rhythmic faculties. . . . I am no musician; I am completely ignorant of musical technique; yet here I was, prey to a development in several parts more complicated than any poet could dream. . . .
>
> But in the case I am speaking of, my movement in walking became in my consciousness a very subtle system of rhythms, instead of instigating those images, interior words, and potential actions which one calls *ideas*.[35]

It would be mistaken to equate Valéry's description of the creative process with Yeats's experiments in automatic writing and unconscious creation.

[33] Valéry, "Concerning *Le Cimetière marin*," in *The Art of Poetry*, trans. Denise Folliot (New York: Pantheon Books, 1958), p. 146.

[34] Valéry, "Poetry and Abstract Thought," in *The Art of Poetry*, p. 75.

[35] Ibid., pp. 60-62. Valéry further confirms this explanation of poems originating in rhythm in the case of *Le Cimetière marin* and *La Pythie* later in the same essay (pp. 80-81). This essay was first delivered as a lecture at Oxford in 1939. Ten years earlier, Valéry had given much the same account of the origin of these two poems (though without naming them) in a lecture before the Société Française de Philosophie (see Valéry, "The Creation of Art," in *Aesthetics*, trans. Ralph Manheim [New York: Pantheon Books, 1964], pp. 130-31.)

No major critic of the last two hundred years has been more insistent on the absolute necessity for conscious control over the writing of poetry than Valéry. Nevertheless, he avers here that a poem begins in certain rhythmic regularities, in patterns of sound that precede any "abstract thought" whatsoever.[36] Interestingly, his experience corresponds precisely to that of Hopkins in composing "The Wreck of the Deutschland." Writing to Canon Dixon nearly three years after the poem was begun, Hopkins said: "I had long had haunting my ear the echo of a new rhythm which now I realised on paper" (L. II, 14). The poem comes into existence only when "realised on paper," but it originates in the rhythm "haunting" the poet's ear. Hopkins and Valéry set about fulfilling the Mallarmean poetic ideal (which Valéry himself said was the essence of Symbolism): "Cet acte de juste restitution qui doit être le nôtre, de tout reprendre à la musique."[37]

Valéry did not discover Hopkins until late in life, long after his own poetics had been formulated under the decisive influence of Mallarmé. But when he did, it was with a shock of recognition:

> I discover, this morning, on the table that serves as a night table, a volume of poems by a certain Gerard Manley Hopkins—with notes by Robert Bridges. I open it and decipher a bit with a vague grudge and without sensing that I am about to find "twenty minutes" of light. The preface by Charles Williams seems to me ordinary or absurd—at first—then it wakes me, and I grope through the poems and the notes by Bridges. Then I see clearly how all this suits me, *situates* me. An excellent guide that justifies my idea of poetry—which now comes clear to me. I understand also the Englishman's contempt for our poetry, and all the poverty of the French way of teaching language—total negligence of the element of music.[38]

[36]The paradoxical goal of Valéry's poetics, to recapture the chance experiences of inspiration (like the rhythm which came to him while walking) in moments of the greatest lucidity, is best illustrated in the following passage which concerns the "peculiar and private 'method'" he evolved for writing poetry during the twenty-year hiatus in his own poetic career: "I shall mention only two points of this method, and I should certainly be hard put to it to explain it further. Here is the first: *As much consciousness as possible*. And here is the second: *Try by conscious will to achieve a few results similar to those interesting or usable ones which come to us (out of a hundred thousand random events) from mental chance*" (Valéry, "Memoirs of a Poem," in *The Art of Poetry*, p. 120).

[37]Quoted in Valéry, *The Art of Poetry*, p. 331.

[38]Valéry, *Leonardo, Poe, Mallarmé*, p. 383. That the same poetic might recur in Valéry and Hopkins without either one's knowing the work of the other should not have surprised Valéry. In his notebooks he once remarked: "Two men unknown to each other, at different times and in different places, with no contact literary or other, arrive at the same *idea*. So, in Baudelaire's *Mon Coeur mis à nu* I find a very particular thought on love, which is also (to a fraction) found in a manuscript of Leonardo's, and which Baudelaire *could not* have known" (Valéry, *Leonardo, Poe, Mallarmé*, pp. 336-37).

Valéry's admiration was immediate. Hopkins presented to him a virtual mirror image of his conception of poetry, a justification of his intuitions about the relation of verse to music. Indeed there is much common ground in their respective poetics, much that is similar above all in their understanding of the origin of poetry in music.

In an essay entitled, appropriately enough, "De la diction des vers," Valéry remarks on the similarity of spoken verse to song: "In studying a piece of poetry to be spoken aloud, one should never take as a beginning or point of departure ordinary discourse or current speech, and then rise from the level of prose to the desired poetic tone; on the contrary, I believed one should start from song, put oneself in the attitude of the singer, tune one's voice to the fullness of musical sound, and from that point descend to the slightly less vibrant state suitable to verse."[39] Valéry's opinion about the proper mode of poetic recitation surely derives from his belief, one that has had considerable vitality and persistence in the Western tradition,[40] that language and song were originally identical. While discussing the concept of ornament in one of his early essays on Leonardo, Valéry has this to say about the original unity of speech and melody:

> Or think of speech and its primitive melody, the separation of words from music and the branching development of each; on the one hand, the invention of verbs, of writing, the *figurative* complexity of language that becomes possible, and the occurrence—so peculiar—of abstract words; on the other hand, the system of tones rendered more flexible, extending from the voice to the resonance of materials, enriched by harmony, then varied by the use of different timbres. And finally let us observe a similar progression in the structures of thought, first through a sort of primitive psychic onomatopoeia, then through elementary symmetries and contrasts, till it reaches the ideas of substances, metaphors, a faltering sort of logic, formalism, entities, metaphysical concepts.[41]

Like Rousseau and Vico, Valéry believes that language was originally musical, hence, the recurrent emphasis in his criticism on the genesis of

[39]Valéry, "On Speaking Verse," in *The Art of Poetry*, p. 162.

[40]On the persistence of this tradition in the West, see Jacques Derrida, *Of Grammatology*, trans. Gayatry Chakravorty Spivak (Baltimore: Johns Hopkins University Press, 1976), part 2 "Nature, Culture, Writing," and the discussion of Derrida and Saussure in chapter 2 below. The contemporary theory of poetry most vigorously adumbrating and attempting to revive this tradition (which never truly vanished) is that of Harold Bloom. See his *Poetry and Repression* (New Haven: Yale University Press, 1976), pp. 1-27; and "The Breaking of Form," in *Deconsctruction and Criticism* (New York: Seabury Press, 1979), pp. 1-27.

[41]Valéry, "The Method of Leonardo," in *Leonardo, Poe, Mallarmé*, pp. 44-45.

poems from simple rhythmic patterns and on the intimate relationship of poetry to music. If language was melodic at its inception, then poetry structured according to musical patterns is somehow in touch with the natural origin of language, perhaps even, to put it in Heideggerian terms, with Being itself.

This view of the natural bond between language and music accords well with many of Hopkins's comments on the subject. In a letter to Bridges late in life, he observed: "This old heptachord scale is founded deeply in nature; it can never perish; and it is it which compels us to use and to find so much pleasure in the dominant seventh, in other words in a chord having for its two extreme notes the extremities of the heptachord scale" (L. I, 235). The heptachord is the basis of the Dorian rhythm in Greek poetry, so that Hopkins in effect affirms the same principle of symmetry between poetry and music asserted by Valéry, Mallarmé, and the other Symbolists. And in a passage from another letter to Bridges, Hopkins pushes the origin of music and poetry back one step further —both originate in the primitive rhythms of dance:

> I think I remember that Patmore [in his "Prefatory Study on English Metrical Law"] pushes the likeness of musical and metrical time too far—or, what comes to the same thing, not far enough: if he had gone quite to the bottom of the matter his views would have been juster. He might remember that for more than half the years music has been in the world it had perhaps *less* time than verse has, as we see in plainchant now. . . . Strict musical time, modern time, arose from dance music. Now probably verse-time arose from the dance too. The principle, whether necessary or not, which is at the bottom of both musical and metrical time is that everything should go by twos and, where you want to be very strict and effective, even by fours. But whereas this is insisted on and recognised in modern music it is neither in verse. . . . Now this principle of symmetry and quadrature has, as I think, been carried in music to stifling lengths and in verse not far enough and both need reforming; at least there is room, I mean, for a freer musical time and a stricter verse-prosody. [L. I, 119-20]

Had Valéry known this letter (he almost certainly did not), he might have noted with a certain satisfaction the intuition that poetic form originated in the dance. His beautiful Socratic dialogue, "L'Ame et la danse," is devoted to this problem. In what sense, Valéry appears to ask there, can aesthetic form be represented by the image of the dancer? The entire dialogue is an attempt to render in language the formal perfection of the dancer whose performance the speakers behold while they are talking. The movement of the dancer, in the words of Eryximachus, "Becomes an universal model."[42] For both Valéry and Hopkins, there is some principle in nature that determines the formal beauty of a work of art, and this principal is above all apparent in the rhythms of dance and music. The language of poetry strives, often in vain, to reproduce the formal unity, the almost pure sonority that precedes and dominates the semantic level of the poem.[43]

There is, obviously, a contradiction here, one that Valéry recognizes in his own attempt to represent the movements of the dancer in language. As Socrates says of Athikte: "She is the pure act of metamorphosis."[44] But language itself is not a pure act, nor is poetry, nor the written text of Valéry's dialogue, a reproduction in visual characters of the movements of the dancer or the sounds of a song. Eryximachus's question is a telling one: "What clearer expression of dancing do you want than dancing itself?"[45] Appropriately, Athikte, the dancer, having completed her performance, has the final words of the dialogue: "Refuge, refuge, O my refuge, O Whirlwind! I was in thee, O movement—outside all things."[46] The essence of the dance is movement, transition, metamorphosis, which can only be imitated, never duplicated, in the relative stasis of the poetic text. Movement, the dance, is "outside all things," including language. The ideal goal of a language or a poetry identical with the "condition of music" is the vanishing point of aesthetic speculation for Hopkins and

[42] Valéry, "Dance and the Soul," in *Dialogues*, trans. William McCausland Stewart (New York: Pantheon Books, 1956), p. 39.

[43] Valéry himself makes the explicit comparison between his theory of poetry and the formal properties of the dance in his essay, "Philosophy of the Dance," in *Aesthetics*, pp. 207-8. Ralph Freedman has commented well on the image of the dance as a metaphor for Valéry's conception of poetry: "By becoming someone other than himself (the embodiment of himself in the poem through the creative act), yet by resolutely remaining himself, the poet has composed an analogue of his own acts of consciousness yet has set them apart from himself through the formal elaborations. The figure of the dance as an activity that exists through space but displaces space, and that has no 'reality' (i.e., no purposive function) outside itself, is the most profound metaphor for Valéry's response to the perennial disjunction between the artist's self and the form which he has made yet which must ultimately exist by itself" (Freedman, "Paul Valéry," in *Modern French Criticism*, p. 31). The dance also provides the central figure for Victor Brombert's analysis of Valéry's prose style, "Valéry: The Dance of Words," *Hudson Review* 21 (1968): 675-86. On the centrality of this metaphor in modern poetry, see Erich Heller, "Yeats and Nietzsche," in *The Disinherited Mind*, expanded ed. (New York: Harcourt, Brace, Jovanovich, 1975), pp. 344-45.

[44] Valéry, "Dance and the Soul," in *Dialogues*, p. 48.

[45] Ibid., p. 44.

[46] Ibid., p. 62.

Valéry. For poetry is always *in* language, hence, it is always written. Such an "absolute" or "pure poetry" envisioned by Valéry, Mallarmé, Stevens, and Hopkins stands at the limits of language itself, at that point where language ceases to be itself and passes into song.[47]

What strikes one most forcibly in both Hopkins and Mallarmé (to a lesser extent and in a somewhat different way in Valéry—I am thinking of the twenty-year hiatus in his poetic career during which Valéry neither wrote nor published poetry, devoting himself instead to the study of mathematics and physics)[48] is the burden placed upon them by the severity of their poetics. For Valéry, the problem posed by Mallarmé hinged on the extremity of his *askesis* and the way in which this determined the shape of his poetic career. Writing to Henri Mondor, Mallarmé's biographer, Valéry says:

> For me [the essential problem posed by Mallarmé's life and art] amounts to this: how and whence was born that strange and un-shakable *certainty* on which Mallarmé was able to found his whole life, his renunciations, his unparalleled daring, his so triumphantly successful undertaking to recreate himself, to make himself in fact the

[47] Geoffrey Hartman has elucidated the irreducible tension in Valéry's poetics between language and the desire to transcend language through music. Citing Valéry's belief that the "lyric wishes to become, one might say, pure melody," Hartman finds in the poetic enactment of this desire "a 'prolonged hesitation' between sound and sense, or formal and referential values" (Hartman, "Valéry's Fable of the Bee," in *The Fate of Reading and Other Essays* [Chicago: University of Chicago Press, 1975], pp. 244, 246). I would merely add that this "prolonged hesitation" leads finally to the vanishing of any "referential values" whatsoever in the poet's recognition that his language can speak nothing but its own being. As Gérard Genette has said: "Valéry soupçonnait bien des pages de littérature d'avoir pour toute signification: 'Je suis une page de littérature'" (Genette, "La littérature comme telle," in *Figures*, vol. 1 [Paris: Editions du Seuil, 1966], p. 254). Hartman himself comes close to saying as much when he remarks: "That Valéry's art is doubled by a reflection on art only helps him to constitute the latter as the allegorical or deeper meaning" ("Valéry's Fable," p. 226). But it can be argued that the double reflection of allegorical meaning finally constitutes for Valéry (and for Hopkins and Mallarmé) the poem's *only* meaning, as I have argued in my reading of "The Windhover" in the introduction.

[48] Jean Hytier has pointed out that Valéry's "period of silence" has been much exaggerated, that Valéry continued to think about and to compose poetry after 1892, though he wrote almost no poetry between 1900 and the composition of *La Jeune Parque* in 1912 (see Hytier, *La Poétique de Valéry*, 2nd ed. [Paris: Armand Colin, 1970], pp. 7-8). But as Genette has perceptively noted, the threat of falling into absolute silence was the very condition of Valéry's existence as a writer: "Si toute oeuvre moderne est de quelque façon hantée par la possibilité de son propre silence, Valéry fut, et reste apparemment le seul écrivain qui n'ait pas vécu cette possibilité comme une menace, une tentation portant sur l'avenir, mais comme une expérience antérieure, préliminaire, peut-être propitiatoire" (Genette, "La littérature comme telle," in *Figures*, 1: 254).

man of a work he did not accomplish and which he knew could not be accomplished.[49]

Valéry makes it absolutely clear that the genius of Mallarmé was intimately related to his renunciation, that "Mallarmé the sterile, Mallarmé the precious, Mallarmé the obscure" was "also Mallarmé the most fully conscious, Mallarmé the most highly perfected, Mallarmé the most pitiless toward himself of all who have ever held the pen." Mallarmé's poetic achievement is inseparable from his asceticism; the two were the mutually constitutive elements of his special accomplishment as a writer, who, Valéry says, "provided me with an idea of writing that was in some way transcendent, a *limit-idea* or archetype of its value and power."[50]

The similarity to Hopkins is unmistakable. It might be objected that Hopkins's *askesis*, unlike Mallarmé's, was religiously motivated, but this misses the mark in two ways. In the first place, it ignores the powerful pressures against writing that were largely self-created by Hopkins. It was not simply the discipline of the Jesuits that made Hopkins's career so plagued by suffering and the inability to write. Anyone who reads the letters of the Dublin period, the devotional writings, and the terrible sonnets, and then compares these painful accounts of Hopkins's trials during the period of his priesthood with the equally painful notations in his early diaries of acts of self-denial and renunciation can only conclude that the ascetic, self-denying impulse was an integral part of Hopkins's personality long before he became a Jesuit. In addition, it simply will not do to make an arbitrary distinction between Hopkins's Catholicism and Mallarmé's less orthodox but no less demanding or profoundly felt religious feeling for art. Speaking of the achievement of the Symbolist poets, Valéry confessed that to describe their condition one was compelled "to use terms only to be found in the vocabulary of religious ecstasy." What impressed him most about Mallarmé was the latter's "singular consuming mysticism," which perhaps reached its zenith in *Un Coup de dés*, a poem Valéry could only discuss in religious terms: "A text, I thought, all clarity and enigmas, as tragic or as indifferent as might be; that spoke and did not speak; woven of multiple meanings, assembling order and disorder; proclaiming a God as forcefully as it denied Him."[51] Such a characterization might without undue violence to its intention be applied to these lines:

[49]Valéry, *Leonardo, Poe, Mallarmé*, p. 426.
[50]Ibid., p. 251.
[51]Ibid., pp. 230, 296, 311.

We hear our hearts grate on themselves: it kills
To bruise them dearer. Yet the rebellious wills
Of us we do bid God bend to him even so.

And where is he who more and more distills
Delicious kindness?—He is patient. Patience fills
His crisp combs, and that comes those ways we know. [P, 102]

The poet's struggle with the divinity who resists and denies his right to create is the central drama of modern poetry. In the writings of Hopkins and Mallarmé can be found all the ecstasy and all of the tragedy of that drama.[52]

[52]The *agon* of the modern poet's career is an old and familiar (perhaps too familiar) story. Its history might reasonably be said to begin with the publication of Verlaine's *Les Poètes maudits* in 1884, though clearly it has roots in the career of Baudelaire, and behind him Poe and the late eighteenth and early nineteenth-century cult of terror which can be seen in the development of the Gothic novel. Though I am not unmindful of this tradition, and though I am undoubtedly heir to it and thus influenced by it in ways I only barely comprehend, I wish to suggest a more precise significance for the poet's *askesis* in Hopkins and Mallarmé than the familiar figure of the "cursed poet" provides. The most rigorous recent theoretician of poetic *askesis* is Harold Bloom, who takes the word from Pater (see *Poetry and Repression*, p. 19). His interpretation of the poet's career as being realized in a severe asceticism is exemplary: "The final product of the process of poetic *askesis* is the formation of an imaginative equivalent of the superego, a fully developed *poetic will*, harsher than conscience, and so the Urizen in each strong poet, his maturely internalized aggressiveness" (Bloom, *The Anxiety of Influence* [New York: Oxford University Press, 1973], p. 119). Hopkins's word for what Bloom calls "poetic will" is *arbitrium*, which he associates insightfully, though painfully and in the end destructively, with Satan (see below, chapter 3).

II HOPKINS AND THE THEORY OF LANGUAGE

Men believe that their reason is lord over their words, but it happens, too, that words exercise a reciprocal and reactionary power over our intellect. Words, as Tartar's bow, shoot back upon the understanding of the wisest, and mightily entangle and pervert the judgement.

> —*Francis Bacon*

"When I use a word," Humpty Dumpty said, in rather a scornful tone, "it means just what I choose it to mean—neither more nor less."

"The question is," said Alice, "whether you can make words mean so many different things."

"The question is," said Humpty Dumpty, "which is to be master—that's all."

> —*Lewis Carroll*

MALLARMÉ'S AND HOPKINS'S INTEREST IN the history and development of ordinary language is well known. Hopkins's etymological notes in his early diaries and Mallarmé's *Les Mots anglais* can be cited as compelling evidence of their common interest in historical philology. But it was Valéry who, despite his much inferior technical knowledge of historical linguistics to the other two, made the most explicit statement of the theory of the linguistic sign that informs the poetics of all three: "Linguistic signs are absolutely distinct from their meaning: no rational or empirical path can lead from sign to meaning. Thus a man is never incoherent to himself, at the moment of thinking; his language is his own; he is compelled to understand himself."[1] Valéry's aperçu appears in a review of Michel Bréal's *La Sémantique* published in *Mercure de France* (January 1898), a startling date when one considers how much it anticipates in Saussure's semiology and in Wittgenstein's notion of "language games." But what appears to be a remarkable anticipation of some of the most

[1]Paul Valéry, *Aesthetics*, trans. Ralph Manheim (New York: Pantheon Books, 1964), p. 253.

important developments in twentieth-century language study is merely the extension of certain principles more or less systematically developed in the philological studies of the nineteenth century, specifically of the work in historical linguistics that centered on the important question of the origin of language.

In 1866, the Société Linguistique declared in its bylaws that it would not accept any communication dealing with the question of the origin of language. It thereby officially ended, so it seemed, all inquiry into the thorny problem that had plagued many of the most illustrious—Rousseau, Herder, Vico, and Condillac—and not a few of the less celebrated—Süssmilch, Maupertuis, and Lord Monboddo—minds of the previous century.[2] A similar declaration was made in 1873 by Alexander J. Ellis, president of the Philological Society of London: "I conceive such questions [concerning the origin of language] to be out of the field of philology proper. . . . We shall do more by tracing the historical growth of one single work-a-day tongue, than by filling wastepaper baskets with reams of paper covered with speculations on the origin of all the tongues."[3] Despite the worthy efforts of the London and Paris societies, a fair amount of paper continued to be expended on this subject, some of it, no doubt, worthy of the fate to which Ellis relegated it, but some deserving serious consideration even now. No less a figure than Sir Edward B. Tylor took up the problem in his *Anthropology* (1871). Having discussed the imitative and interjectional theories at some length, he concluded: "All we have a right to say is that, from what is known of man's ways of choosing signs, it is likely that there was always some kind of fitness or connexion which led to each particular sound being taken to express a particular thought. This seems to be the most reasonable opinion to be held as to the famous problem of the Origin of Language."[4] A far cry from the oracular pronouncements of Vico, Herder, and Rousseau, and yet Tylor's seemingly cautious conclusion nevertheless addresses directly the very question that the London and Paris societies had attempted to rule out of court. Nor did Charles Darwin, iterating the opinions of his brother-in-law Hensleigh Wedgwood,

[2]The history of this question in the eighteenth century has been definitively treated by Hans Aarsleff, "The Tradition of Condillac," in *Studies in the History of Linguistics*, ed. Dell Hymes (Bloomington: Indiana University Press, 1974), pp. 93-156. A more diffuse treatment of the same subject can be found in Michel Foucault, *The Order of Things* (New York: Random House, 1970), pp. 78-124.

[3]Quoted in Hans Aarsleff, *The Study of Language in England, 1780-1860* (Princeton: Princeton University Press, 1967), p. 230.

[4]Sir Edward B. Tylor, *Anthropology*, abridged by Leslie A. White (Ann Arbor: University of Michigan Press, 1960), p. 39.

scruple to pronounce boldly on the subject: "I cannot doubt that language owes its origin to the imitation and modification of various natural sounds, the voices of other animals, and man's own instinctive cries, aided by signs and gestures."[5]

Darwin and Tylor typify the enduring fascination with the question of origins that has been a leading characteristic of European thought for the past one hundred years. In their differing but related ways, Nietzsche, Freud, Heidegger, Husserl, Sir James Frazer, D. H. Lawrence, Joyce—virtually the entire constellation of thinkers who come immediately to mind when one invokes the term "modern"—took as their project the illumination of the origins of man. Admittedly, none of these men believed that his work was directed specifically at revealing the origin of language, but the intimate relationship between the origin of language and the origin of man inevitably drew them into the labyrinth that comparative philology had unsuccessfully attempted to seal off once and for all. It is in the context of the general inquiry into the origin of man and the specific theories of the origin of language current in the middle of the nineteenth century that Mallarmé's, but even more Hopkins's, speculations on language must be understood. Hopkins's interest in the origin of language is apparent from his early diaries. Scattered throughout are numerous speculations about the etymologies of words and several remarks about the origin of some words, generally attributed to onomatopoeia. A typical passage occurs in the diary entry for September 24, 1863:

Horn.

The various lights under which a horn may be looked at have given rise to a vast number of words in language. It may be regarded as a projection, a climax, a badge of strength, power or vigour, a tapering body, a spiral, a wavy object, a bow, a vessel to hold withal or to drink from, a smooth hard material not brittle, stony, metallic or wooden, something sprouting up, something to thrust or push with, a sign of honour or pride, an instrument of music, etc. From the shape, *kernel* and *granum*, *grain*, *corn*. From the curve of a horn, κορωνις, *corona*, *crown*. From the spiral *crinis*, meaning ringlets, locks. From its being the highest point comes our *crown* perhaps, in the sense of the top of the head, and the Greek κέρας, horn, and κάρα , head, were evidently identical; then for its sprouting up and growing, compare *keren*, *cornu*, κέρας, horn with grow, *cresco*,

---

[5]Charles Darwin, *The Descent of Man and Selection in Relation to Sex*, 2nd ed., rev. and aug. (New York: D. Appleton & Co., 1896), p. 87.

grandis, grass, great, *groot*. For its curving, *curvus* is probably from the root *horn* in one of its forms. κορωνη in Greek and *corvus, cornix* in Latin and *crow* (perhaps also *raven*, which may have been *craven* originally) in English bear a striking resemblance to *cornu, curvus*. So also γέρανος, *crane, heron, herne*. Why these birds should derive their names from *horn* I cannot presume to say. The tree *cornel*, Latin *cornus* is said to derive its name from the hard horn-like nature of its wood, and the *corns* of the foot perhaps for the same reason. *Corner* is so called from its shape, indeed the Latin is *cornu*. Possibly (though this is rather ingenious than likely, I think) *grin* may mean to curve up the ends of the mouth like horns. Mountains are called *horn* in Switzerland; now we know from Servius that *herna* meant *saxum* whence the Hernici, *Rock-men*, derive their name; *herna* is a horn-like crag. ἔρνος, a shoot, is so called from its horn-like growth. Curiously enough the expression κεράων ἔρνος occurs in Oppian, and another word, ἔρνυξ, in the *Poetics* of Aristotle. Or is it possible that ἔρνος may be so called from its shooting up as, not in the shape of, a horn. Expression. He hath raised up a horn of salvation for us. [J, 4]

One can marvel at Hopkins's astonishingly fertile imagination (he was nineteen when this was written), as he discovers such a wealth of words in Greek, Latin, and English related to the single root "horn." Whether or not Hopkins's speculations on the derivation of words from "horn" are correct in light of current knowledge (he seems to have been well versed in the etymological materials available to him in his own time)[6] is not so important as the principles that underlie his derivations. Hopkins assumes the existence of a primitive root, which he calls "horn," and generates from the various physical aspects of a horn a seemingly limitless variety of words to designate other objects whose shape or function resembles one of the physical characteristics of a horn, and whose pronunciation suggests a phonological affinity with the root word.

---

[6] According to Alan Ward's "Philological Notes" (J, 499-500), Hopkins's principal sources for etymologies were the following: Liddell and Scott's *Greek-English Lexicon* (4th ed., 1855; 5th ed., 1861); Ogilvie's *Imperial Dictionary* (1851); Todd's revision of Johnson's Dictionary (1818); Richardson's *New Dictionary of the English Language* (1836-37); Max Müller's *Lectures on the Science of Language* (1st series, 1861); and Ogilvie and Wedgwood's *Dictionary of English Etymology* (1859-65). It is worth mentioning that Richardson was a disciple of Horne Tooke and that Hopkins was thus indirectly influenced by *The Diversions of Purley*. Omitted from Ward's list, but almost certainly another of Hopkins's sources (see below, note 11) was R. C. Trench's *On the Study of Words* (1851). On the popularity of Trench's work and on his role in the popularization of language study in England, see Aarsleff, *Study of Language in England*, pp. 234-35.

The origin of "horn" itself is unaccounted for. Moreover, the relations between individual etymological lines, for example the series *kernel, granum, grain, corn* and the series *corvus, cornix, crow, raven-craven, cornu, curvus,* remain obscure, perhaps unaccountable, like the origin of "horn" itself. The postulated root gives rise to a nonlinear series of linguistic descendants, families of words that trace their heritage from the parent "horn" but which no longer show clear signs of filiation with each other.[7] The hypothetical character of the whole schema is emphasized in a subsequent note: "See *horn* above. On the other hand the derivation of *granum, grain* may be referred to the head" (J, 5). In these and many similar passages in his early diaries, Hopkins presents neither a straight line of derivation nor a simple and clear origin for a given word or group of words.[8] He describes, rather, a distribution of verbal signs that are related phonologically, morphologically, or semantically, and that can, in some cases, be traced back via different paths to an original etymon. But the etymon itself is only a speculative postulation, a convenient fiction for the origin of words. What Hopkins says of slang, that it is "the application of a term in a metaphorical or whimsical sense" (J, 16), is equally true of root words like "horn."[9]

For some words, however, Hopkins believes that the origin can be determined:

Grind, gride, gird, grit, groat, grate, greet, κρούειν, crush, crash, κροτεῖν etc.

   Original meaning to *strike, rub,* particularly *together.* That which is produced by such means is the *grit,* the groats or crumbs,

[7]The same model of filiation in which traces of original parentage have been obscured is familiar from Darwin's *Origin of Species.* See especially chapter 4, "Natural Selection." The concurrence of biological and linguistic models in the nineteenth century is treated extensively by Foucault in *The Order of Things,* pp. 250-302.

[8]See J, 5, 7, 8, 9, 11, 12, 13, 15, 19, 21, 25, 36, 46, 47. The passage on page 36 is particularly interesting, since it testifies to Hopkins's awareness of the relative positions of Sanskrit, Gothic, and Slavonic in the development of the Indo-European family of languages.

[9]This method, of course, is commonplace in modern comparative linguistics. See the explanation of this procedure given by Saussure: "On ne peut établir la forme primitive d'un signe unique et isolé, tandis que deux signes différents mais de même origine, comme latin *pater,* sanscrit *pitar-,* ou le radical de latin *ger-ō* et celui de *ges-tus,* font déjà entrevoir par leur comparaison l'unité diachronique qui les relie l'une et l'autre à un prototype susceptible d'être reconstitué par induction" (Ferdinand de Saussure, *Cours de linguistique générale,* édition critique préparée par Tullio de Mauro [Paris: Payot, 1972], p. 292. In designating Saussure as the author of the *Cours,* I am of course gliding over the difficult question of the relationship between his thought and the presentation of it made by his students after his death and handed down in the text of the *Cours* (see De Mauro's discussion of these textual problems, *Cours,* pp. 406-9). I am not unmindful of this difficulty, but to confront it in detail here would be an unnecessary distraction from my principal theme, the theory of language in Hopkins.

like *fragmentum* from *frangere*, *bit* from *bite*. *Crumb, crumble,* perhaps akin. To *greet*, to strike the hands together (?). *Greet*, grief, wearing, *tribulation*. *Grief* possibly connected. *Gruff*, with a sound as of two things rubbing together. I believe these words to be onomatopoetic. *Gr* common to them all representing a particular sound. In fact I think the onomatopoetic theory has not had a fair chance. Cf. *Crack, creak, croak, crake, graculus, crackle*. These must be onomatopoetic. [J, 5]

What does it mean to say that words originate in onomatopoeia? To answer this question, it is necessary to consider some of the theories of the origin of language, among them the imitative or onomatopoetic theory, that were current in Hopkins's time and of which he was aware.

Discussions of the origin of language go back at least as far in Western thought as Plato's *Cratylus*, but the crucial questions crystallized in the middle of the eighteenth century into a debate over four principal hypotheses: divine revelation; imitation of animal cries and other sounds in nature (onomatopoeia); repetition of natural human emotional cries (interjectional); and the representation of certain human actions by the primitive grunts men uttered when they got together to accomplish necessary tasks. Max Müller's derisive labels for the last three have served since his time as the most convenient means of distinguishing among them: the "bow-wow" theory; the "pooh-pooh" theory; and the "yo-he-ho" theory.[10]

Though Herder claimed to have disproved the divine revelation hypothesis in his prize essay for the Berlin Academy, *Abhandlung über den Ursprung der Sprache* (1772), the idea retained considerable vitality in the nineteenth century. Writers as divergent in their approaches to language as Trench, Bunsen, Donaldson, and, in a somewhat more complicated way, Renan all proposed a version of the revelation hypothesis.[11] Hopkins, of course, would scarcely have been immune to the attractions of such a theory, which implies a natural and necessary relationship

[10]Max Müller refuted the "bow-wow" and "pooh-pooh" theories in *Lectures on the Science of Language*, 1st series (1861; rpt. New York: Charles Scribner's Sons, 1871), pp. 358-70. Despite Müller's disclaimer that the terms he coined "were not intended to be disrespectful to those who hold the one or the other theory" (*Lectures*, p. 358), it is hard to suppress one's natural amusement when discussing them under such labels. Nonetheless, people in the eighteenth and nineteenth centuries took these ideas seriously, even though it is sometimes difficult for us to do so, particularly with the persistent ring of Müller's appellatives in our ears.

[11]See Richard Chenevix Trench, *On the Study of Words*, rev. ed. (1877; rpt. New York: A. C. Armstrong, 1889), pp. 26-28. Christian Charles Josias Bunsen, *Outlines of the Philosophy of Universal History Applied to Language and Religion* (London: Longmans, 1854), 2: 126-30; John William Donaldson, *The New Cratylus* (London: J. W. Parker, 1839),

between language in its primitive state and the created world. The basic metaphysical assumption of this theory, that language and nature are mirrors reflecting each other in a simple and undistorted manner, must have had a seductive influence over a poet who sought, especially in the nature sonnets of the 1870's, to affirm the immanence of God in creation by miming God's presence in language.[12] Two passages, one from Hopkins's notebooks, the other from his undergraduate essay "Parmenides," confirm this view: "All words mean either things or relations of things: you may also say then substances or attributes or again wholes or parts. E.g., [sic] *man* and *quarter*. To every word meaning a thing and not a relation belongs a passion or prepossession or enthusiasm which it has the power of suggesting or producing but not always or in everyone. This *not always* refers to its evolution in the man and secondly in man historically. . . . for the word is the expression, *uttering* of the idea in the mind"; "To be and to know or Being and thought are the same. The truth in thought is Being, stress, and each word is one way of acknowledging

pp. 13-14, 44-46. I shall discuss the argument of Renan's *De l'Origine du langage* (1848) more thoroughly later. The striking resemblance between a passage in Trench's *On the Study of Words* (p. 350) and a passage in Hopkins's diaries (J, 12) has been remarked by Alan Ward: "Trench's book was of course well known at the time; and it is interesting to note here not only the similarities between some of these explanations and those Hopkins gives, but also a general similarity in style between this passage and similar passages in Hopkins" (J, 514). As I indicate at several points in this chapter (see notes 6 and 13), Hopkins seems to have been familiar with *On the Study of Words*. Particularly during the early period of Hopkins's interest in the origin of language when he was a student at Oxford, Trench's emphasis on words (rather than the structure of language) and his tentative proposal of the revelation hypothesis would have held a special fascination for Hopkins. The similarity of Trench's book to Mallarmé's *Mots anglais* should also be noted.

[12]Hillis Miller has argued that this theory of language as a repetition of God's immanence in the world is, in fact, what Hopkins believed: "For [Hopkins] language originates in a kind of inner pantomime, in fundamental movements of the body and the mind by which we take possession of the world through imitating it in ourselves. Words are the dynamic internalization of the world" (J. Hillis Miller, *The Disappearance of God* [Cambridge: Harvard University Press, 1963], p. 285). Miller's description, however, more closely resembles the imitative or onomatopoetic theory than the theory of divine revelation. As my treatment of Renan and Farrar will show, it is often difficult to separate in any final way some of the conflicting theories of the origin of language. On this point, the immanence of God in creation as evidenced in the mimesis of nature in language, the hypotheses of divine revelation and of onomatopoeia coincide.

Whether or not Hopkins ultimately affirms the immanence of God in the world is an important and complicated point. As I shall argue presently, Hopkins's apparent belief in the imitative theory of the origin of language cannot finally be sustained in the face of opposing tendencies in his writings. Hopkins's life-long desire to establish God's immanence in nature remains, in his poetry and in his theory of language, chimerical and unrealizable. The pressures of contrary theories of language and poetry deconstruct the mimetic theory proposed here.

Being and each sentence by its copula *is* (or its equivalent) the utterance and assertion of it" (J, 125, 129). Hopkins contends here that thought reflects what is (Being), and that language merely mimes thought. The best explanation of the origin of this relationship among language, thought, and Being would seem to be the divine revelation theory of the origin of language. According to this theory, language begins when God imparts the knowledge of creation to man by endowing him with a language (or a language capacity) that reflects the things in the world. This Adamic language is "original" in the etymological sense of the word, which means "to arise," like the sun out of the east. God thus "gives rise to" or originates language in man.[13]

But this postulation of a simple, divine origin of language is not unequivocally affirmed by Hopkins. In a letter dated April 6, 1886, to his friend A.W.M. Baillie, the Egyptologist, Hopkins takes quite another position: "And here consider that in religion more than in language a thing may have no one origin, it may be at the meeting point of many influences. Even words (as they say is shewn in Murray of *allow*) are sometimes two words rolled into one, approximated till they blend meanings. As soon for instance as the Romans settled that Mercury was Hermes, everything told of Hermes was true of Mercury, and so on" (L. III, 266). In the same letter, Hopkins continues this line of reasoning with an extraordinary derivation of the name Aphrodite, which leads him through a maze of sources in Greek, Egyptian, and Syrian mythology to an unsettled conclusion: "Here is more confusion, but also room for enquiry" (L. III, 267). The origin of Aphrodite remains mysterious, lost in the mists of the mythological-linguistic past; the goddess and her name are without unique origin, but are rather "the meeting point of many influences." The result of Hopkins's researches is "confusion," which leaves "room for enquiry," but there is no reason to suppose that further research will achieve clarity and simplicity, that it will, in short, reveal

[13]Cf. Trench: "But the truer answer to the inquiry how language arose, is this: God gave man language, just as He gave him reason, and just because He gave him reason; for what is man's *word* but his *reason*, coming forth that it may behold itself? . . . Here, as in everything else that concerns the primitive constitution, the great original institutes, of humanity, our best and truest lights are to be gotten from the study of the first three chapters of Genesis; and you will observe that there it is not God who imposed the first names on the creatures, but Adam—Adam, however, at the direct suggestion of his Creator. *He* brought them all, we are told, to Adam, 'to see what he would call them; and whatsoever Adam called every living creature, that was the name thereof' (Genesis 2: 19). Here we have the clearest intimation of the origin, at once divine and human, of speech: while yet neither is so brought forward as to exclude or obscure the other" (Trench, *On the Study of Words*, pp. 26-27).

the origin of Aphrodite. The series of letters to Baillie, from which the passages just quoted are taken, beginning in February 1886 and continuing until May 1888 (L. III, 257-94), is filled with similar conjectures on the origin of Greek mythology. The names of gods and customs are traced etymologically through Crete and Phoenicia and back to Egypt, where, Hopkins wishes to demonstrate, Greek civilization originated. But like his youthful etymological notes, these speculations encounter insuperable barriers, blocked passages that lead nowhere and everywhere at the same time. The chimerical quality of Hopkins's search for the origins of Greek mythology in Egypt is especially apparent in a letter to Baillie of February 20, 1887:

> My Egyptian guesses were wild and the children of ignorance, which opens up those possibilities that knowledge wd. close. Still three deserve consideration—Rhadamanthys, Sarpedon, and Aphrodite. Oedipus is the mere suggestion of a possibility. The name may, as you say, be foreign and yet not Egyptian. I did not however overlook this. I knew that much in Greek religion and civilisation came from Asia Minor, a wide region and hitherto little explored. But of two doors, one open, the other locked, we go in by the open one; if inside that we find what we want we leave the locked-up room alone. So of Egypt and Asia. [L. III, 277-78]

Certain knowledge of the origin of Greek mythology stands behind a closed door, though this difficulty does not prevent Hopkins from hypothesizing about what is concealed behind it. But his ideas remain hypothetical, fantastic fictions based on supposed but indemonstrable linguistic and conceptual affinities between Greece and Egypt. In the study of myths and of the words in which they are embodied, the concept of the origin can never be simple, unbroken, univocal, never, in short, original.[14]

If the path leading back to the origin of language through divine revelation is closed off, language must begin, as Herder and others argued, in something characteristically, in fact uniquely, human. Hence, one is

[14]In the review of Bréal's La Sémantique cited earlier, Valéry makes the following observation about the concept of origin: "In every field, origin is an illusion. The search for it, beyond our experience, is purely verbal. This concept of an origin is too strongly attached to all the objects of our knowledge: it leads us to modify them by thought until they are no longer recognizable, that is, to destroy them for the moment; and this might teach us something. But it leads us at the same time to substitute, unconsciously, objects other than the one we modify, for this object itself; and the new objects are at once contemporaneous with the first and supposedly anterior" (Valéry, Aesthetics, p. 243).

led to conjectures about the origin of language like the ones cited earlier
— the imitative or onomatopoetic ("bow-wow"), the interjectional ("pooh-
pooh"), and the concerted action ("yo-he-ho") theories. These theories
were popular in the eighteenth century, and one at least (the imitative)
retained considerable currency in the nineteenth century, notably in two
writers whose work would have been known to Hopkins, Frederic Farrar
and Ernest Renan. Farrar's *Essay on the Origin of Language* (1860), as the
full title indicates, derives from the work of Renan. Farrar's book is
important to the study of Hopkins because he devotes an entire chapter
to the question of onomatopoeia, the result of which is a deep ambivalance
toward the imitative theory akin to Hopkins's own.[15] Early in the *Essay*,
Farrar apparently denies all theories of the origin of language as innate,
as imitative of natural sounds, or as the gift of divine revelation: "We
conclude, then, that language is neither innate and organic; nor a
mechanical invention; nor an external gift of revelation;—but a natural
faculty swiftly developed by a powerful instinct, the result of intelligence
and human freedom which have no place in purely organic functions."[16]
Farrar's hostility toward the imitative hypothesis has the same grounds
as Darwin's enthusiasm for it: It assumes that language is generated by a
form of "mechanical invention," that in effect any species with similarly
structured speech organs could evolve a language. Farrar is completely
opposed to this view of language: "Language may be regarded as the
union of words and grammar, of which words are analogous to matter,
and grammar to form. . . . That which originates language, like that
which originates thought, is the logical relation which the soul establishes
between external things."[17] For Farrar "words" are not at all the same
thing as "language." Words in themselves do not constitute a language,
which is "the union of words and grammar," but they are the stuff out of
which language is made. This distinction between words and language

[15]The editor's note to the passage cited earlier in this chapter in which Hopkins declares
that the "onomatopoetic theory has not had a fair chance" (J, 5) is somewhat misleading on
this point. The note states: "Chapter IV [of Farrar's *Essay*] argues for the 'onomatopoetic
origin of many words and roots,' some of which are also mentioned here by Hopkins"
(J, 294). Farrar explicitly repudiates all theories that propose the invention of language by
mechanical means, including the imitative theory. As I shall argue below, Farrar qualifies
this position somewhat, but only by making a distinction between "words" and "language."

[16]Frederic W. Farrar, *An Essay on the Origin of Language, Based on Modern Researches
and Especially on the Works of M. Renan* (London: J. Murray, 1860), pp. 31-32. The
similarity to Chomsky's theories of language and mind, his postulation of an innate language
capacity, and his stipulation for linguistic creativity as evidence of human freedom are
striking. See Noam Chomsky, *Cartesian Linguistics* (New York: Harper & Row, 1966).

[17]Farrar, *Essay*, p. 62.

allows Farrar to recover, in a modified form, the onomatopoetic theory by contending that primitive words, or roots, (but not language itself) originated in onomatopoeia:

> We may now state our belief that *almost all* primitive roots were obtained by *Onomatopoeia, i.e.,* by an imitation with the human voice of the sounds of inanimate nature. Onomatopoeia sufficed to represent the vast majority of physical facts and external phenomena; and nearly all the words requisite for the expression of metaphysical and moral convictions were derived from these onomatopoeic roots by *analogy* and *metaphor.*[18]

While individual roots arose through the imitation of natural sounds, language proper came into existence only when these roots were rendered figurative, when "analogy" and "metaphor" created concepts not directly derived from man's experience of the physical world. Language, for Farrar, is a system of specifiable formal relations among originally unrelated root words.

Farrar clarifies the relationship between the mechanical and intellectual functions of language some pages later: "Metaphor—the transference of a word from its usual meaning to an analogous one— is the intellectual agent of language, just as onomatopoeia is the mechanical agent."[19] Words were first produced mechanically (by onomatopoeia), but language, properly speaking, came into existence only when the primitive onomatopoetic roots were transformed by the intellectual agency of metaphor. Language can be said to be the union of these two mechanical and intellectual agents, of onomatopoetic roots and metaphor. Mentioning Rousseau along with Herder and a host of others as propounders of the onomatopoetic theory, Farrar follows them in declaring that language (though not necessarily words) is originally and irreducibly figurative.

While it can be argued that the dissemination of Farrar's opinions on the origin of language was not vast, even in his own country, the same cannot be said of Renan. His works were widely read, especially in England and Germany, and his views on language were extremely influential—if not always correct, even by mid-nineteenth-century standards.[20] Renan first published *De l'Origine du langage* in 1848; in

[18]Ibid., pp. 62-63.

[19]Ibid., p. 117.

[20]No certain evidence exists to prove that Hopkins read Renan's works, but he must have been exposed to Renan's ideas from a variety of sources. For example, H. P. Liddon's Bampton Lectures, *The Divinity of Our Lord*, contain numerous references to Renan's *Vie*

1858, he reissued the piece and appended a lengthy preface in which he explained his purpose in writing the essay originally and surveyed the work published on the subject in the ensuing decade. Early in the preface, Renan contends that the unity of language "comme celle de l'humanité elle-même" is the result of diverse causes which came together to form "une oeuvre indivise et spontanée."[21] Language was generated spontaneously and in common among all men, but to say so is not to assume the existence of a single primitive tongue as the source of all existing languages. This is the view of Müller and Bunsen vigorously contradicted by Renan: "Donc, si l'aryen primitif n'avait été qu'une branche d'un ensemble plus étendu, on retrouverait la trace de l'affinité des langues indo-européennes avec d'autres groupes de langues. Or, MM. Bunsen et Müller n'ont pas, selon nous, réussi à prouver qu'une telle affinité existe, et sans vouloir préjuger de l'avenir de la philologie, il est permis de dire que l'on n'entrevoit pas à l'horizon l'ombre même d'une démonstration sur ce point capital."[22] Renan's quarrel with Müller and Bunsen is that they posit without being able to prove the original unity of all languages, even of the Semitic and the Aryan families. Renan rejects this notion not only as unproven but unprovable. For Renan, as for Hopkins, the origin of language stands at the vanishing point of intellectual inquiry. The further one pushes the investigation into origins back in time, the more the originary moment recedes from sight, so that all one can discern is a multiplicity of origins. In Renan's argument, the limits of this inquiry are defined by the fundamental division among language families typified by the irreducible differences between the Semitic and the Aryan families.

---

de Jésus. Hopkins attended these lectures (see J, 135, 136, 138) and would undoubtedly have been interested in Renan's book, one of the most renowned examples of the Higher Criticism. Hopkins could have been acquainted with Renan's linguistic works through Max Müller, whose writings he knew as an undergraduate and in whom he continued to be interested later in life (see J, 36, 530; L. III, 262-63). In the preface to the second edition of *De l'Origine du langage* (1858), Renan attacked Müller and his mentor Christian Bunsen for their hypothesis concerning the Turanian family of languages and for asserting the original unity of all languages (see Ernest Renan, *De l'Origine du langage,* in *Oeuvres Complètes,* édition définitive établie par Henriette Pischari [Paris: Calmann-Lévy, 1958], 8: 27-33). Müller responded with an unfavorable review of the second edition of Renan's *Histoire générale et système comparé des langues sémitiques* entitled "Semitic Monotheism" (1860), in which he challenged Renan's assertion that the Semitic race was monotheistic in character and thus fundamentally distinct from the Aryan (see Max Müller, *Chips from a German Workshop* [1867; rpt. New York: Scribner, Armstrong & Co., 1873], 1: 337-74). Hopkins could also have learned about the work of Renan from Trench's *On the Study of Words,* which mentions *De l'Origine du langage* and quotes approvingly a long passage from the *Histoire* (see Trench, *On the Study of Words,* ed. cit., p. 28).

[21]Ernest Renan, *Oeuvres Complètes,* 8: 22.
[22]Ibid., 8: 33.

But like Hopkins, Rousseau, Farrar, and Herder, Renan cannot resist his own nostalgia for a primitive language common to all men. This language, not surprisingly, is onomatopoetic:

> L'imitation ou l'onomatopée paraît avoir été le procédé ordinaire d'après lequel ils formèrent les appellations. La voix humaine étant à la fois *signe* et *son*, il était naturel que l'ont prît le son de la voix pour signe des sons de la nature. . . .
>
> La langue des premiers hommes ne fut donc, en quelque sorte, que l'écho de la nature dans la conscience humaine. Les traces de la sensation primitive se sont profondément effacées, et il serait maintenant impossible, dans la plupart des langues, de retrouver les sons auxquels elles durent leur origine; toutefois, certains idiomes conservent encore le souvenir des procédés qui présidèrent à leur création. Dans les langues sémitiques et dans l'hébreu en particulier, la formation par onomatopée est très sensible pour un grand nombre de racines, et pour celles-là surtout qui portent un caractère marqué d'antiquité et de monosyllabisme. Bien que plus rare ou plus difficile à découvrir dans les langues indo-européennes, l'onomatopée perce encore dans les rameaux même les plus cultivés de cette famille.[23]

To assert that the roots of existing languages were generated by onomatopoeia is to postulate an original language quite as fantastic as any proposed by Müller and Bunsen. Any attempt to discover the origin of language is bound in involve one in the kind of contradictory hypotheses proposed by Renan. For all his superior sophistication and his more thorough knowledge of the historical development of the Indo-European and Semitic language families, Renan's account of the origin of language is no more compelling or coherent than the theories he criticizes. The theory of onomatopoeia, however attractive and commonsensical it appears as an account of the origin of language, turns out to be as much a fiction as the hypotheses it claims to refute. The onomatopoetic theory, even in the hands of its most eminent partisans, can only offer a fabulous or fictional account of the origin of language. One must understand Hopkins's enthusiasm for this theory and the etymological speculations that led him to it in light of these considerations.

To return to Hopkins's etymological notes, it is worth examining further the principles that govern his perception of the affinities between different words. The series that Hopkins attributes to an onomatopoetic origin, "*Crack, creak, croak, crake, graculus, crackle*" (J, 5), or the series

[23] Ibid., 8: 70-71.

"Drill, trill, thrill, nostril, nese-thirl" (J, 10), or the series *"Shear, shred, potsherd, shard"* (J, 12)—in these and in virtually all the groups of etymologically related words recorded by Hopkins in his diaries, the affinitive principles are primarily phonological (hence, the attractiveness of the imitative theory). Though Hopkins searches for semantic relations that will link the words more closely, sound correspondences are what suggest similarity in the first instance. The words seem to be variations on a single root, a primitive original sound (*Gr* in *crack, creak,* etc.) from which the elements in the series ray out in a distribution of potentially infinite complexity. But what are these roots? Where do they come from? What leads Hopkins to assume their existence in the first place? These questions lead one back once again to the problem of the origin of language, and to Max Müller, for whom the discovery of roots represented the final goal of all inquiries into this problem.[24]

Müller began to answer the question of the origin of language by first establishing its limits: "The only way to answer, or at least to dispose of [the origin of language], is to consider the nature and origin of roots; and we shall then have reached the extreme limits to which inductive reasoning can carry us in our researches into the mysteries of human speech."[25] Müller's project is not extreme or unusual in the context of mid-nineteenth-century philology. What he says about the nature of these roots, however, is quite startling: "Roots therefore are not, as is commonly maintained, merely scientific abstractions, but they were used originally as real words."[26] This is the point at which Müller diverges from the mainstream of philology in his day and which makes his work especially pertinent to the discussion of Hopkins's thoughts on language. Müller later suggests that the primitive roots still evident as the constitutive elements in all languages can be numbered between 400 and 500. These roots are not "interjections, nor are they imitations. They are *phonetic types* produced by a power inherent in human nature."[27] All of this sounds reasonable enough, though it is undoubtedly speculative and cannot be rigorously demonstrated. But when Müller undertakes to explain what he means by "phonetic types," the discourse takes an extraordinary turn:

[24] As Taylorian Professor of modern European languages (1854-1868), professor of comparative philology (1868-1900), and oriental sublibrarian at the Bodleian (1865-67), Max Müller was a prominent figure at Oxford when Hopkins was a student from 1863-1867. The explicit references to Müller in Hopkins's diaries and letters (see note 20), and Müller's considerable reputation in Oxford and throughout Europe suggest that Hopkins was well acquainted with his theories of language.

[25] Max Müller, *Lectures on the Science of Language,* p. 342.

[26] Ibid., p. 358.

[27] Ibid., p. 384.

There is a law which runs through nearly the whole of nature, that everything which is struck rings. Each substance has its peculiar ring. We can tell the more or less perfect structure of metals by their vibrations, by the answer which they give. Gold rings differently from tin, wood rings differently from stone; and different sounds are produced according to the nature of each percussion. It was the same with man, the most highly organized of nature's works. Man, in his primitive and perfect state, was not only endowed, like the brute, with the power of expressing his sensations by interjections, and his perceptions by onomatopoeia. He possessed likewise the faculty of giving more articulate expression to the rational conceptions of his mind. That faculty was not of his own making. It was an instinct. . . . The number of these *phonetic types* must have been almost infinite in the beginning, and it was only through the same process of *natural elimination* which we observed in the early history of words, that clusters of roots, more or less synonymous, were gradually reduced to one definite type. Instead of deriving language from nine roots, like Dr. Murray, or from *one* root, a feat actually accomplished by a Dr. Schmidt, we must suppose that the first settlement of the radical elements of language was preceded by a period of unrestrained growth, —the spring of speech—to be followed by many an autumn.[28]

Müller has been stigmatized ever since he wrote this passage as the leading proponent of the "ding-dong" theory of the origin of language. With some reservations concerning the propriety of the label employed, the judgment is not entirely unjust. And after all, Müller was scarcely more charitable when he popularized the terms "bow-wow" and "pooh-pooh" to describe the imitative and interjectional theories.[29] Difficult as it may be to take seriously any theory called "ding-dong," Müller's ideas claim some attention, particularly since, of all the theories of the origin of language that retained currency in Hopkins's time, Müller's comes closest to explaining Hopkins's own understanding of language.

Müller's theory takes up the ancient problem in Western thought, discussed at length by Socrates in the *Cratylus*, of the relation between words and things. In the passage just quoted, Müller contends that the

[28]Ibid., pp. 384-85.
[29]Müller later tried to deny his advocacy of "ding-dongism," (see his "Reply to Mr. Darwin," *Contemporary Review* [1875], rpt. in *Chips from a German Workshop* [New York: Charles Scribner's Sons, 1900], 4: 452), but the onerous lable seems to have stuck (see Aarsleff, *Study of Language in England*, pp. 229-30).

human capacity for language is analogous to the differentia that distinguish substances—gold, wood, tin—in nature. Each substance, Müller claims, has its individual sound or tone, a unique ring that distinguishes it from all other substances. At its origin, language consisted of "phonetic types," a nearly infinite variety of sounds representing the variety of substances and objects that men perceived in nature. The natural "ringing" of substances in the world was reproduced in the differentiated sounds that made up the primitive roots of language.

It has often been observed that the characteristic heavy alliteration, assonance, and end rhymes in many of Hopkins's poems establish unexpected relationships among widely divergent things and qualities in nature.[30] Long series of phonologically linked words like "daylight's dauphin, dapple-dawn-drawn," "Selfwrung, selfstrung, sheath-and shelterless," and "Stigma, signal, cinquefoil" (P, 69, 98, 58) appear everywhere in Hopkins's poetry. Related to the lists of etymologically linked words in Hopkins's diaries, they are the auditory repetition of the poet's experience of the world. Each slight change in the pattern of sound from word to succeeding word marks a shift in the poet's perception, as he sees things anew in each succeeding moment. But the altered perceptions expressed in the sound changes in each series are not innate in the poet (as Müller contends words are not innate in mankind); they arise from the analogous "ringing" of objects in nature. Hopkins's conception of this analogy between language and nature is best expressed in his sonnet, "As kingfishers catch fire":

As kingfishers catch fire, dragonflies draw flame;
   As tumbled over rim in roundy wells
   Stones ring; like each tucked string tells, each hung bell's
Bow swung finds tongue to fling out broad its name;
Each mortal thing does one thing and the same:
   Deals out that being indoors each one dwells
   Selves—goes itself; *myself* it speaks and spells
Crying *What I do is me: for that I came.* [P, 90]

As has often been noticed, the poem proclaims Hopkins's notion of "inscape," which he defined in a letter to Coventry Patmore (November

---

[30]Notably by Hillis Miller in *The Disappearance of God*. His treatment of rhyme in Hopkins is exemplary. For a brief but important discussion of the relation of rhyme to meaning in Hopkins (with a significant comparison to Milton's rejection of rhyme in *Paradise Lost*), see Geoffrey H. Hartman, "The Voice of the Shuttle," in *Beyond Formalism*, (New Haven: Yale University Press, 1970), pp. 345-47.

7, 1886) as "species or individually-distinctive beauty of style" (L. III, 373).[31] As if in emulation of Max Müller, the poem proposes a theory of language in which "each mortal thing" cries out its special qualities, "finds tongue to fling out broad its name." This natural language of things is essentially what Müller meant by his "phonetic types," his "almost infinite" number of primitive roots from which all language developed. Hopkins's poetry mimes or reproduces or imitates the ringing sounds of nature.

Just as the innumerable variety of primitive roots has been reduced to the finite figure of 400 or 500, in a comparable manner, the alliterated and rhymed words in Hopkins's poems are related by similarities in sound to some root word or sound from which they derive. But this root is never a true origin, merely a beginning, a convenient starting point that generates the series. The closing lines of "That Nature is a Heraclitean Fire and of the comfort of the Resurrection" typify this aspect of Hopkins's poetry: "This Jack, joke, poor potsherd, | patch, matchwood, immortal diamond, / Is immortal diamond" (P, 106). The phonological changes begin with the transformation of the vowel from "Jack" to "joke" and proceed through a series of further changes to the concluding repetition of the phrase "immortal diamond." The poem proposes an affinity among these words without giving any hint about the ultimate source or ground of their relation. Like the diary note from which at least part of the series comes—"*Shear, shred, potsherd, shard.* The *ploughshare* that which divides the soil. *Share* probably=divide. *Shrad* also, which is same as shred" (J, 12)—the first word represents an arbitrary beginning point

[31]Hopkins's coining of this term is not without etymological warrant, or at least so he believed (see the letters to Baillie of March 10 and April 6, 1887, in L. III, 284-86). Inscape is related to Hopkins's concept of "selving" and to his understanding of the word "sake" as he employs it in the sonnet on Henry Purcell. Hopkins explained this idiosyncratic usage in a letter to Bridges dated May 26, 1879: "It is the *sake* of 'for the sake of,' *forsake, namesake, keepsake.* I mean by it the being a thing has outside itself, as a voice by its echo, a face by its reflection, a body by its shadow, a man by his name, fame, or memory, *and also* that in the thing by virtue of which especially it has this being abroad, and that is something distinctive, marked, specifically or individually speaking, as for a voice and echo clearness; for a reflected image light, brightness; for a shadow-casting body bulk; for a man genius, great achievements, amiability, and so on. In this case it is, as the sonnet says, distinctive quality in genius" (L. I, 83). Hopkins's coining of terms like "inscape" and "sake" resembles his postulation of etymons like "horn" for the original form from which a wide range of related words derives. These words signify concepts that provide a theoretical structure for a system of relations evident in language or in nature, but a system lacking any visible or identifiable principle of coherence. "Inscape," "horn," and "sake" offer a hypothetical origin for the coherence that Hopkins seeks but cannot locate in nature and in language. Hopkins's neologisms may also be compared to such Derridean coinages as *différance, dissémination,* and *déconstruction.*

without authority (philological or ontological) over the succeeding elements. The "immortal diamond" (Christ) does not originate in "This
Jack" (presumably the poet), though the two are related to each other as
the beginning and ending of a series. The source of their relation, the
structure that governs the progression of sounds from "Jack" to "immortal
diamond" is wholly unaccountable. "Jack" and "immortal diamond" are
somehow analogous, in the same way that language and nature are
somehow analogous, but the only way to describe this analogy is by
means of such apparently random distributions of words as "Jack, joke,
poor potsherd" and so on.

The most powerful tradition of commentary on Hopkins has asserted
that he was a poet of immanence. This tradition is fairly represented in
the following quotation from Hillis Miller's *The Disappearance of God:*

> Beginning with a sense of his own isolation and idiosyncracy, Hopkins
> turns outside himself to nature, to poetry, and to God. Gradually he
> integrates all things into one chorus of many voices all singing, in
> their different ways, the name of Christ. Poetry is the imitation and
> echo of this chorus. Even the poet, by virtue of his share in the
> common nature, is assimilated into the melody of creation. The
> inscapes of words, the inscapes of nature, the inscape of the self can
> be expressed at once as the presence of Christ. . . . The inspiration of
> poetry is always, in one way or another, the poet's affective response
> to the omnipresence of Christ.
>
> The isolation of the poet in his selftaste has turned out to be
> apparent, not real, and Hopkins' early experience of the absence of
> God has been transformed into what is, in Victorian poetry, an
> almost unique sense of the immanence of God in nature and in the
> human soul.[32]

Miller's own reading grapples incessantly with this persistent strain in
Hopkins's writing, evading again and again the tendency to simplify
Hopkins's poetic achievement to a mere celebration of nature and God's
participation in His creation. But in the end Miller cannot avoid what
Harold Bloom terms an "idealizing," "canonical" interpretation of Hopkins.
In Miller's reading, Hopkins, driven virtually to despair near the end of
his life, was thrown back upon the irresistible action of grace, guaranteed
by Christ's incarnation, death, and resurrection. By a passive acceptance
of grace, Hopkins salvaged his belief in the power of God to redeem the

[32]Miller, *The Disappearance of God*, pp. 323-24.

world, including the crushed and suffering soul of the poet. Not surprisingly, this salvation of the poet and the participation of this world in transcendence is figured in the being of Christ expressed by St. John as *Logos:*

> Each created thing is a version of Christ, and derives its being from the way it expresses Christ's nature in a unique way. All things rhyme in Christ.
>
> This vision of Christ as the common nature is the culmination of Hopkins' gradual integration of the world. Christ is the model for all inscapes, and can vibrate simultaneously at all frequencies. He is the ultimate guarantee for the validity of metaphor. It is proper to say that one thing is like another only because all things are like Christ.[33]

Miller's reading is powerfully logocentric, as many of the best interpretations of Hopkins have tended to be. My own reading of Hopkins attempts a transumptive revision of the logocentric, idealizing, canonical tradition in Hopkins criticism. What this tradition omits most tellingly is the theory of language toward which Hopkins groped in his journals and which he produced in his poetry. The language of Hopkins's poetry is generated by analogical correspondence in which the poem produces a heterocosm, a world structurally parallel to but ontologically distinct from objects and events in nature. Hopkins's poetry is neither immanential nor incarnational; it is not a form of *gnosis*.[34] For Hopkins, poetry is the structuration of language, and language is structured by laws and relations

---

[33] Ibid., p. 313. The drama (and the special strength) of Miller's interpretation does not lie in his recognition of the importance of the Incarnation and the Real Presence to Hopkins's poetry and ontology, but in his moving portrayal of Hopkins's gradual descent into spiritual impotence in his later years. Hopkins ends up, Miller argues, a passive recipient of God's grace, clinging desperately to "the comfort of the Resurrection" (*The Disappearance of God*, p. 358). Miller thus says, without quite saying it, what I wish to say more explicitly: that Hopkins's poetic career was a failure, that his poetry did not achieve the repetition of the *Logos* he heroically strove for. Like Christ, his model poet, Hopkins "was doomed to succeed by failure; his plans were baffled, his hopes dashed, and his work was done by being broken off undone. However much he understood all this he found it an intolerable grief to submit to it. He left the example: it is very strengthening, but except in that sense it is not consoling" (L. II, 138). The special shape of Hopkins's career as a poet derives from his increasingly extravagant stratagems for realizing a poetic language which he suspected from the first (witness the evidence of the etymological speculations in his early diaries) was chimerical.

[34] The most thoroughly elaborated reading of Hopkins's poetry as incarnational and as gnostic knowledge is James Finn Cotter's *Inscape* (Pittsburgh: University of Pittsburgh Press, 1972). A cogent refutation of this tendency to read Hopkins as a poet of immanence is Jacob Korg's "Hopkins's Linguistic Deviations," *PMLA* 92 (October 1977): 977-86. Drawing upon Foucault's argument in *The Order of Things* (pp. 280-300) concerning the emergence

that are intrinsic to itself. Poetry mimics language (as the ending of "That
Nature is a Heraclitean Fire" mimics one of the etymological series in
Hopkins's notebooks), and language mimics itself. No such thing as a
natural language (an originally imitative or interjectional language) is
available to the poet, or even recoverable by means of the most elaborate
and ingenious etymologies. The paths of etymological research, like the
paths of aesthetic speculation, lead one back via circuitous routes to an
origin that is never original, to a source for language that is always
contained within language itself. Hopkins's poetry is bound within what
Nietzsche perceptively called the prison-house of language, a place of
confinement no reading of Hopkins can safely neglect to explore.

The entities of linguistic form are of "algebraic" nature and
have no natural designation; they can therefore be designated
arbitrarily in many different ways.

— *Louis Hjelmslev*

In what sense is language a prison-house? What restrictions and
barriers does the writer confront in language? Another way of asking this
question is to inquire into the general problematic of writing in Hopkins's
texts. As I have shown in discussing the debate over the origin of language
in the mid-nineteenth century, there is considerable impetus in Hopkins's
writings toward a theory of natural language. In the eighteenth and nine-

---

in the nineteenth century, especially in Mallarmé, of a concept of language as an autonomous
system, Korg argues that Hopkins's deviation from ordinary linguistic usage marks a step
toward the realization of such an autonomous language for poetry. But Korg draws back
from the radical implications of his own line of reasoning, and thus, to my mind, vitiates the
strength of his argument when he contends that the language of Hopkins's poetry retains a
certain mimetic or referential function: "This process does not go so far in Hopkins's poetry
as it does in Mallarmé's, for the former remained loyal to the reality of things while
pursuing the reality of language" (p. 980). As the argument of these first two chapters has
shown, it is not at all certain that Hopkins does not go as far as Mallarmé in seeking a non-
representational language for poetry, though it is true that Hopkins continued to grope for
the representational language that Korg attributes to his poetry. In fairness to Hillis Miller,
it should be noted that in some of his recent essays he has begun to give more emphasis to
the theme of language in Hopkins's writings and thus to revise in a serious way his earlier
reading of Hopkins's poetry of immanence (see J. Hillis Miller, "The Linguistic Moment in
'The Wreck of the Deutschland,'" in *The New Criticism and After*, ed. Thomas Daniel
Young, the John Crowe Ransom Memorial Lectures 1975 [Charlottesville: University Press
of Virginia, 1976], pp. 47-60; and idem, "Nature and the Linguistic Moment," in *Nature
and the Victorian Imagination*, ed. U. C. Knoepflmacher and G. B. Tennyson [Berkeley and
Los Angeles: University of California Press, 1977], pp. 440-51).

teenth centuries, such a language was often thought to be the original human tongue, the language spoken by Adam and Eve in paradise or the language invented by primitive man. In either case, this language was thought to be natural and original, the source from which all currently existing languages had descended by means of mechanisms that were rapidly being discovered by linguistic scientists. Hopkins's enthusiasm for the imitative theory and his implicit endorsement of Max Müller's "ding-dong" theory typify an important tendency in nineteenth-century language studies to assume the existence of an original language that was more intimately in harmony with nature than the artificial languages of modern times. This belief in the existence of a natural language can be traced to eighteenth-century theories of the origin of man, above all to Rousseau, Vico, and Herder, and to many less well-known but not necessarily less important figures as well. The important point is that numerous writers well into the nineteenth century, including Hopkins, believed that language (and man, who invented or perhaps was given it) had a simple, natural, unproblematic origin. Moreover, this language was often assumed to be spoken rather than written; writing was generally thought to have come into existence after speech and in imitation of it.

In Hopkins's writings, one can find considerable support for the view that speech is prior to and more natural than writing. Much that he says about his own poetic practice and about poetry in general gives spoken language a special privilege. Consider, for example, this paragraph from a letter to Bridges written October 11, 1887:

> I will enclose the sonnet on Harry Ploughman, in which burden-lines (they might be recited by a chorus) are freely used: there is in this very heavily loaded sprung rhythm a call for their employment. The rhythm of this sonnet, which is altogether for recital, not for perusal (as by nature verse should be) is very highly studied. From much considering it I can no longer gather any impression of it: perhaps it will strike you as intolerably violent and artificial. [L. I, 263]

Hopkins wishes to justify to Bridges the use of sprung rhythm, which he elsewhere characterizes as "the most natural of things," "the rhythm of common speech and of written prose, when rhythm is perceived in them," and "the rhythm of all but the most monotonously regular music" (P, 48-49). For Hopkins, sprung rhythm is more natural than common or "running" rhythm; it derives above all from spoken language and from music. The sonnet cannot, properly speaking, be read; it can only be recited. Speech possesses special qualities for Hopkins; it adds a dimension to the poem (rhythm) absent in visual perusal. Speech is full and natural;

writing is empty and artificial. Speech completes and fulfills what writing only indicates and suggests. Writing is "intolerably violent and artificial."

This passage has numerous analogues in Hopkins's writings about poetry,[35] and a powerful case can be made for reading Hopkins's own poetry as an attempt to imitate spoken language.[36] Moreover, Hopkins's speculations on a general theory of language tend also to valorize speech over writing and to assume that written language: 1) is an attempt to represent the sound of spoken language visually; 2) evolves under the pressure of phonological variations. The following passage from a letter to Baillie of April 28, 1886, shows clearly the theories of language and linguistic change that dominated Hopkins's thinking:

Curtius and others do hold that θ, ϕ, χ were all $t+h$ $p+h$, $k+h$. I am not posted in the controversy. In modern Greek they are th (as in English th proper . . .), ph or f, and ch as in German etc. Curtius knows this, but says the change took place later than classical times, later than the Christian era I think. The evidence available on this and like heads is difficult to deal with and seems at first sight to prove more than it does. For instance Tahuti | $\theta\epsilon\acute{v}\theta$ or $\theta\omega\theta$ seems conclusive that θ was $t+h$. But it is not. For what the first θ appears to prove the second as much appears to disprove. It does rather more, for an initial θ and especially in the name of a god was very congenial to a Greek tongue but a final θ quite the contrary. It may therefore be (and, I think myself, was) the case that the Egyptian t here sounded to the Greeks like their θ and that the h was omitted (for the Greeks did not write it in the body of a word, excepting certain grammarians, and especially in the word $\tau\alpha\acute{\omega}\varsigma$ | peacock; but there it was, I think, rather a w than an h) and then the two vowels became the diphthong ϵv or (in the form T'huti) ω.

It is hard for us to conceive that $t+h$ cd. become th and in English they scarcely could, because the position of the organs has to be changed so much; but I find in myself a tendency to turn *make haste* into ma-khaste, the change of position being slighter. [L. III, 272-73]

The procedures Hopkins follows here were (and are) common and accepted in historical linguistics. Ever since the work of Bopp and Grimm,

---

[35] See especially J, 267, 289; L. I, 160, 192, 280; L. II, 354, 380-81.

[36] The case has been made most vigorously by James Milroy in his book *The Language of Gerard Manley Hopkins* (London: André Deutsch, 1977) and by Father Ong in his essay "Hopkins's Sprung Rhythm and the Life of English Verse," in *Immortal Diamond*, ed. Norman Weyand, S.J. (New York: Sheed & Ward, 1949).

German philologists had emphasized the importance of phonetics in describing the mechanisms of linguistic change. Hopkins is clearly familar with the general principles of sound change and knows at least some of the contemporary work on aspirates done by Curtius and others. In one sense, Hopkins is merely following the accepted linguistic theory of his day, but that he would accept a theory of linguistic change based on sound changes has more far-reaching consequences than one might at first suppose.

In a much earlier piece of writing, dated by House and Storey around 1873-1874 (see J, xxvii), Hopkins comments in detail on the characteristic qualities of poetry and verse, claiming once again that the primary model for written language is speech, that poetry and verse are nothing more than the record of spoken language:

> Poetry is speech framed for contemplation of the mind by the way of hearing or speech framed to be heard for its own sake and interest even over and above its interest of meaning. Some matter and meaning is essential to it but only as an element necessary to support and employ the shape which is contemplated for its own sake. . . . Verse is . . . speech wholly or partially repeating the same figure of sound. Now there is speech which wholly or partially repeats the same figure of grammar and this may be framed to be heard for its own sake and interest over and above its interest of meaning. Poetry then may be couched in this, and therefore all poetry is not verse but all poetry is either verse or falls under this or some still further development of what verse is, speech wholly or partially repeating some kind of figure which is over and above meaning, at least the grammatical, historical, and logical meaning. [J, 289]

This passage is incredibly rich and has rightfully elicited much commentary. It apparently justifies a reading of Hopkins's poetry that privileges speech over writing by making the sounds and rhythms of spoken language into a key for deciphering the enigmas of the written record. But though the passage does indeed tend in this direction, Hopkins at the same time renders such a procedure impossible. Poetry and verse are certainly forms of speech, but spoken language does not provide a key or a code for resolving the ambiguities of written language. The "figure" that is repeated in verse stands "over and above meaning, at least the grammatical, historical, and logical meaning." But what other "meaning" can there be? What kind of "contemplation" does Hopkins intend? Does the interpretive activity simply come to an end when confronted by the

sound of poetic statement? Just what is "speech framed to be heard for its
own sake"?

Hopkins's special sense of the word "sake" must be recalled: "I mean
by it the being a thing has outside itself, as a voice by its echo, a face by
its reflection, a body by its shadow, a man by his name, fame, or memory,
and also that in the thing by virtue of which especially it has this being
abroad, and that is something distinctive, marked, specifically or individually speaking" (L. I, 83). "Speech framed to be heard for its own
sake" is thus formed by its own intrinsic structures, but at the same time
it depends upon the hearing and the intepretive powers of the auditor. To
say that poetry and verse "employ some kind of figure which is over and
above meaning" does not halt interpretation; quite the contrary, it transforms interpretation into an endless activity without temporal or even
logical limits. For Hopkins, poetry is speech, and speech is, paradoxically,
a kind of writing.

This strange dialectic of speech and writing has been treated in great
detail by Jacques Derrida in *Of Grammatology*. Derrida's explication of
Saussure's doctrine of the sign and his elaboration of the concept of the
text (apropos of Rousseau) establish the boundaries for the critical
exploration of writing and speech and make explicit the difficulties
involved in reading a written text. Derrida begins his critique of Saussure
by quoting the preliminary distinction made by Saussure between language and writing: "Langue et écriture sont deux systèmes de signes
distincts; l'unique raison d'être du second est de représenter le premier;
l'objet linguistique n'est pas défini par la combinaison du mot écrit et du
mot parlé; ce dernier constitue à lui seul cet objet."[37] As Derrida shows,
this apparently simple and necessary separation of language from writing

---

[37]Ferdinand de Saussure, *Cours de linguistique générale*, p. 45. A few paragraphs later,
apropos of the confusion among early comparative linguists between language and writing,
we find: "La langue a donc une tradition orale indépendante de l'écriture, et bien autrement
fixe; mais le prestige de la forme écrite nous empêche de le voir. Les premiers linguistes s'y
sont trompés. . . . Bopp lui-même ne fait pas de distinction nette entre la lettre et le son; à le
lire, on croirait qu'une langue est inséparable de son alphabet. Ses successeurs immédiats
sont tombés dans le même piège; la graphie *th* de la fricative *þ* a fait croire à Grimm, non
seulement que ce son est double, mais encore que c'est une occlusive aspirée" (p. 46).
Saussure here criticizes the very theory explained by Hopkins in the letter to Baillie
previously quoted. Hopkins took his information from Georg Curtius (as the letter states),
who was the teacher of Saussure and also of Karl Brugmann, one of the principal Neo-
Grammarians whose work Hopkins knew (see L. III, 192-93; on Brugmann, Curtius, and
Saussure, see *Cours*, p. 412, n. 31). The connection between Hopkins's and Saussure's
theories of language is therefore not at all tenuous but is based upon their common reading
and training in the writings of some of the more prominent linguists of the second half of
the nineteenth century.

has enormous consequences for the new science of signs, semiology, inaugurated by Saussure. When Saussure says that the sole purpose of writing is to represent language (by which he means, Derrida explains, spoken language), he has made an ontological statement about language and has established the limits of linguistic science. Saussure recognizes only two systems of writing, ideographic or alphabetic, and believes that anterior to both is speech. Speech is a language that is original and natural, the key to interpreting writing:

> Thus a science of language must recover the *natural*—that is, the simple and original—relationships between speech and writing, that is, between an inside and an outside. It must restore its absolute youth, and the purity of its origin, short of a history and a fall which would have perverted the relationships between outside and inside. Therefore there would be a *natural order* of relationships between linguistic and graphic signs, and it is the theoretician of the arbitrariness of the sign who reminds us of it.[38]

The effect of this move in Saussure is to make writing subservient to speech, for writing is merely the convenience men adopt to preserve language. Writing is not language but only represents language graphically. Language truly resides in speech, of which writing is but a pale and inadequate image.

Derrida subsequently argues that the privileging of speech over writing apparent in Saussure, and in the structuralist tradition that grows out of his work, notably in the work of Lévi-Strauss, is not a peculiarity of the Saussurean text but is among the most firmly embedded concepts in the Western tradition of thought. Derrida calls this recurrent tendency "logocentrism" (or, alternatively, "phonocentrism") and identifies it as the crucial determinant of all metaphysical speculation in the West from Plato to Heidegger. In opposition to logocentrism and to the model of a natural bond between writing and speech, Derrida proposes a new concept of writing (*écriture*) in which this natural bond is sundered. What remains of language in Derrida's critique is a field of dispersed signs without what he calls "the transcendental signified," that is to say, without a fixed and invariant key to the production of meaning. All that language presents is a text, a point Derrida makes most trenchantly in his reading of Rousseau:

> *There is nothing outside of the text* [there is no outside-text; *il n'y a pas de hors-texte*]. . . . In what one calls the real life of these existences

[38]Derrida, *Of Grammatology*, trans. Gayatry Chakravorty Spivak (Baltimore: Johns Hopkins University Press, 1976), p. 35.

of "flesh and bone," beyond and behind what one believes can be circumscribed as Rousseau's text, there has never been anything but writing; there have never been anything but supplements, substitutive significations which could only come forth in a chain of differential references, the "real" supervening, and being added only while taking on meaning from a trace and from an invocation of the supplement, etc. And thus to infinity, for we have read, *in the text*, that the absolute present, Nature, that which words like "real mother" name, have always already escaped, have never existed; that what opens meaning and language is writing as the disappearance of natural presence.[39]

Derrida's strategy is to liberate interpretation from a slavish subservience to received techniques of reading in which certain signifiers (in the case of Rousseau, his mother and her effect upon his subsequent development as a man; in the case of language, speech) are designated as the primary determinants of meaning in a text. Any text must be interpreted by a reader who immerses himself in the text's language and produces its meaning by his interpretive activity. For Derrida, the production of meaning is an ongoing process, such that no text is ever closed and completely determined either by the author himself or by any reading, just as, for Saussure, language perpetually changes and cannot be arbitrarily arrested in its development. Derrida's term, *écriture*, comes to stand for a system or structure of signifiers that is radically "textual," that is to say, always in need of interpretation, of reading:

> The writer writes *in* a language and *in* a logic whose proper system, laws, and life his discourse by definition cannot dominate absolutely. He uses them only by letting himself, after a fashion and up to a point, be governed by the system. And the reading must always aim at a certain relationship, unperceived by the writer, between what he commands and what he does not command of the patterns of the language that he uses. This relationship is not a certain quantitative distribution of shadow and light, of weakness or of force, but a signifying structure that critical reading should *produce*.[40]

[39]Ibid., pp. 158-59.

[40]Ibid., p. 158. In subsequent work, Derrida characterizes a text as a sort of systematic instability, a structure of relations that consistently eludes any attempt to describe and dominate it: "Un texte n'est un texte que s'il cache au premier regard, au premier venu, la loi de sa composition et la règle de son jeu. Un texte reste d'ailleurs toujours imperceptible. La loi et la règle ne s'abritent pas dans l'inaccessible d'un secret, simplement elles ne se livrent jamais, au *présent*, à rien qu'on puisse rigoureusement nommer une perception" (Jacques

Thus, in the case of language, interpretation cannot simply refer a written text back to the spoken language that the text supposedly represents. Speech is not the signified of the signifier writing, for there is no signified in language which is fixed, invariant, and changeless through time. There is only the chain of signifiers that the reader interprets afresh with each new reading. In Derrida's terms, all language, even speech, is always already writing.

Derrida's theory of writing and reading as the ontologically unconditioned differentiation of textual signifiers and his extension of this textual theory to include all productions of language (all signifying structures, of which language is the most familiar) presents in an inverted form the theory of poetry and writing that I wish to explore in Hopkins's poems. A certain congruence between Hopkins's poetic practice and Derridean theory will emerge, though only through the unmasking of Hopkins's apparent and persistent logocentrism. Though I shall finally argue that Hopkins's poetry realizes a theory of writing not unlike the Derridean theory of the text, the drama of his poetic career was sustained by his continual and simultaneous attraction and resistance to precisely such a theory. This attraction and resistance is registered in the poems themselves, but it also appears in his comments upon the special difficulties presented to the reader by his poems. Throughout the letters to his family and friends in which he discusses these difficulties, Hopkins continually draws attention to the importance of speaking, reciting, and even singing his verse. For example, he instructs Bridges in a letter of December 11, 1886, on "Spelt from Sibyl's Leaves": "Of this long sonnet

---

Derrida, *La dissémination* [Paris: Editions du Seuil, 1972], p. 71). The most thorough, though somewhat critical, treatment of Derrida's theory of textuality to date is Edward W. Said's "The Problem of Textuality," *Critical Inquiry* 4 (Summer 1978): 673-714. On Derrida and the question of reading literary texts, see Alan Bass, "'Literature'/Literature," in *Velocities of Change*, ed. Richard Macksey (Baltimore: Johns Hopkins University Press, 1974), pp. 341-53.

Cf. also the recent characterization of the disfiguring and dismantling mechanisms of structuration in a text by Paul de Man: "We call *text* any entity that can be considered from such a double perspective: as a generative, open-ended, non-referential grammatical system and as a figural system closed off by a transcendental signification that subverts the grammatical code to which the text owes its existence. The 'definition' of the text also states the impossibility of its existence and prefigures the allegorical narratives of this impossibility. . . . A text is defined by the necessity of considering a statement, at the same time, as performative and constative, and the logical tension between figure and grammar is repeated in the impossibility of distinguishing between two linguistic functions that are not necessarily compatible. It seems that as soon as a text knows what it states, it can only act deceptively, like the thieving lawmaker in the *Social Contract*, and if a text does not act, it cannot state what it knows. The distinction between a text as narrative and a text as theory also belongs to this field of tension" (Paul de Man, *Allegories of Reading* [New Haven: Yale University Press, 1979], p. 270).

above all remember what applies to all my verse, that it is, as living art should be, made for performance and that its performance is not reading with the eye but loud, leisurely, poetical (not rhetorical) recitation, with long rests, long dwells on the rhyme and other marked syllables, and so on. This sonnet shd. be almost sung" (L. I, 246).

Hopkins's interest in musical structure is well known.[41] What led him to study music, in particular the theory of composition, was his belief that poetry and music share a common foundation in certain principles of nature. This belief in the correspondence of music and poetry to natural laws can be seen in two letters, separated by some seven years in time, in which Hopkins proposes similar principles underlying the structure of the Italian sonnet and the rhythm of plain chant. The first is a letter to Canon Dixon in which Hopkins explains at length the numerical ratios upon which the sonnet form is based and goes on to state dogmatically: "And even the rhymes, did time allow, I could shew are founded on a principle of nature and cannot be altered without loss of effect" (L. II, 72). The second is to Bridges and is concerned with, among other things, natural versus artificial recitative: "The only good and truly beautiful recitative is that of plain chant; which indeed culminates in that. It is a natural development of the speaking, reading, or declaiming voice, and has the richness of nature; the other is a confinement of the voice to certain prominent intervals and has the poverty of an artifice" (L. I, 280). In both passages, Hopkins links human productions (poetry and song) to phenomena in nature. When he says of "Spelt from Sibyl's Leaves" that it "shd. be almost sung," he is appealing to a theory of poetic structure founded upon formal principles evident in nature.[42] There are in nature, Hopkins believed, principles of symmetry and harmony governing the sequences of sound that the human ear recognizes as music. Poetry, when it achieves genuine beauty, reproduces those sequences.

Certainly it sounds strange to characterize Hopkins's work as "natural," for his poetry strikes the reader at once as highly mannered and stylized to the point of eccentricity. Hopkins himself recognized this and

[41] Hopkins's musical theories and his exercises in composition are intelligently discussed by John Stevens in an appendix to the House and Storey edition of the *Journals* entitled "Gerard Manley Hopkins as Musician" (J, 457-97). Stevens draws attention to the similarity between the theory of poetry evident in some of Hopkins's letters to Bridges and Hopkins's musical practice.

[42] A further indication of Hopkins's belief in the principles of symmetry and order in nature is his lengthy conjecture (near the end of the letter to Bridges just cited) on the hexagonal structure of the cells of the honeycomb constructed by wild bees. Hopkins concludes thus: "But grant in the honey bee some principle of symmetry and uniformity and you have passed beyond mechanical necessity; and it is not clear that there may not be some special instinct determined to that shape of cell after all and which has at the present

defended his mannerism to Bridges: "No doubt my poetry errs on the side of oddness. I hope in time to have a more balanced and Miltonic style. But as air, melody, is what strikes me most of all in music and design in painting, so design, pattern or what I am in the habit of calling 'inscape' is what I above all aim at in poetry. Now it is the virtue of design, pattern, or inscape to be distinctive and it is the vice of distinctiveness to become queer. This vice I cannot have escaped" (L. I, 66). Here is the central paradox of Hopkins's theory of poetry. In seeking to reproduce the natural structures of spoken language, to capture the inscape of speech in poetry, Hopkins is compelled to adopt the most exorbitant stratagems of poetic style: odd, irregular rhythms; heavy alliteration; curious, often imperfect rhymes; unusual diction; and an entire system of special markings for accent and rhythm to aid the reader in recitation. Hopkins once wrote to his mother, apropos of the accentual markings in "The Wreck of the Deutschland": "[Father Henry Coleridge] wants me . . . to do away with the accents which mark the scanning. I would gladly have done without them if I had thought my readers would scan right unaided but I am afraid they will not, and if the lines are not rightly scanned they are ruined" (L. III, 138). Poetry attempts to reproduce speech but does so only imperfectly, so Hopkins wished to insert accentual markings to clarify the reading of the text and bring his writing closer to the spoken language he wished to represent. (In addition, Hopkins used a system of indentation in "The Wreck of the Deutschland" to mark the number of stresses in each line.) The sprung rhythm that Hopkins employs and must mark to make it evident to the reader "is the native and natural rhythm of speech, the least forced, the most rhetorical and emphatic of all possible rhythms, combining, as it seems to me, opposite and, one wd. have thought, incompatible excellences, markedness of rhythm—that is rhythm's self—and naturalness of expression" (L. I, 46). Sprung rhythm is natural and yet it must be marked, something that the reader would fall into merely by speaking but nevertheless so elusive that he would miss it if it were not indicated by a system of notation. Hopkins recognizes the antinomy of speech and writing and attempts to overcome it, but his device for reproducing the "natural rhythm of speech" produces yet

---

stage of the bee's condition, nothing to do with mechanics, but is like the specific songs of cuckoo and thrush" (L. I, 281). This passage can be instructively compared with a similar pronouncement by Ruskin on the instincts of the creative imagination: "Thus we may reason wisely over the way a bee builds its comb, and be profited by finding out certain things about the angles of it. But the bee knows nothing about those matters. It builds its comb in a far more inevitable way. And, from a bee to Paul Veronese, all master-workers work with this awful, this inspired unconsciousness" (John Ruskin, *The Works of John Ruskin*, ed. E. T. Cook and Alexander Wedderburn, Library Ed., 39 vols. [London: G. Allen, 1903-1912], 5: 122).

another system of writing. Though Hopkins may protest that his "verse is less to be read than heard" (L. I, 46), it is only by reading that the precise rhythms he intends can be understood. Hopkins's poetry, like all texts, can never be spoken; it can only be read and interpreted. The speech Hopkins wishes to reproduce is forever vanishing before the horizon of the reader's attention, leaving in its wake traces of itself that constitute the poetry Hopkins wrote.

Nor do the accentual markings that Hopkins left in his manuscripts resolve the ambiguity of the reading process by giving a definitive and final indication of how his poems are to be recited. The problem is well illustrated by the opening lines of "The Wreck of the Deutschland." Following Hopkins's suggestions in manuscripts of the poem, W. H. Gardner scans the first two lines thus:

> Thóu màstering mé
> Gòd! gíver of breáth and bréad. [P, 257]

The indentation dictates two strong stresses in the first line and three in the second. The rhythms of ordinary speech suggest, as Gardner indicates, that "giver," "breath," and "bread" all be accented. But that leaves "God" with at most a secondary stress, though surely it is the most important word in these first two lines and ought, one would think, to be given more accentual strength. Furthermore, though one can see why Gardner chooses to give primary stress to "me" in the first line, an equally plausible reading, one that corresponds to the rhythms of plain chant so much admired by Hopkins, would place the primary stress on the first syllable of "mastering" (this would also facilitate accenting "God" in the next line).[43] It would not even be impossible, save for the injunction that the first line's indentation would indicate only two stresses, to stress all three words in the opening line of the poem and "God" at the beginning of the second line. Perhaps this makes the first line and a half sound a bit grandiose, but the subject and tone of the entire stanza is intended to place the poet and the reader at the highest pitch of religious enthusiasm. Like the opening notes of Beethoven's Fifth Symphony, four strongly accented words at the beginning of this poem announce the gravity and the passion that the poem is going to realize.[44]

[43] This reading of the scansion is proposed by Elisabeth Schneider in *The Dragon in the Gate* (Berkeley and Los Angeles: University of California Press, 1968), pp. 75-76.

[44] Cf. Mallarmé's manifesto for a radically new kind of writing: "Un jet de grandeur, de pensée ou d'émoi, considérable, phrase poursuivie, en gros caractère, une ligne par page à emplacement gradué ne maintiendrait—il le lecteur en haleine, la durée du livre, avec appel à sa puissance d'enthousiasme: autour, menus, des groupes, secondairement d'après leur importance, explicatifs ou derivés—un semis fioritures" (Mallarmé, *Oeuvres Complètes*, [Paris: Bibliothèque de la Pléiade, 1945], p. 381).

Rather than providing the reader with a definitive key to the interpretation of his poetry, Hopkins's accentual markings introduce yet another signifying structure that modifies and in turn is modified by the signifying structures produced by the words themselves. Attempting to recapture the presence of spoken language, Hopkins is compelled to proliferate systems of writing. What he achieves is not the representation of spoken language, but the production of a text in the rigorous though radically unstable conception given that term by Derrida. Hopkins's search for a natural signifying structure to represent speech discloses the painful truth that the presence of speech eludes the poet, leaving him with only the dead letter of his writing. As Hopkins's poetic career unfolded after "The Wreck of the Deutschland," the melancholy recognition that poetry is and can only be writing came to dominate his thoughts more and more, finally to the exclusion of poetry itself.

III   SELF AND TEXT: THE PROBLEMATIC OF WRITING

> . . . for men live Tropes and Figures as well as speak them.
> —*Samuel Shaw*, Words Made Visible

ONE OF THE MOST PERSISTENTLY TROUBLESOME questions raised by Hopkins's writings is the conflict, for which he himself suffered in the extreme, between his vocation as a priest and his desire to write poetry. But this is perhaps to phrase the problem too narrowly, since for Hopkins poetry was but one form of writing (though the form at which he especially excelled) among many that he practiced. Though at times it seems necessary to make distinctions among the various kinds of writing Hopkins produced—poetry, journals and diaries, sermons and devotional writings, and letters—looked at in another way, all the various documents that have survived (and some that have not—I am thinking of Hopkins's "slaughter of the innocents") can be read and studied as a single body of writing. For what does it mean to say that Hopkins wrote? Were writing a poem, making an entry in his journal, composing a sermon, and penning a letter essentially separable activities with different regularities and different spiritual significances for him? Obviously, in some cases they were, though in many important instances the lamentations expressed in letters to friends, the mental anguish recorded in his diary, and the poems produced during the same period are all but indistinguishable, not only in tone and in the subject treated, but even in the very words themselves. The way to approach Hopkins (and perhaps all writers), then, is to consider the general problematic of writing that his texts not only propose but enact in their unfolding.

The question of what constitutes a text, how texts are produced, and how they are sustained and disseminated has been the subject of much critical activity in recent years. It would be impossible, and essentially pointless in the context of the present discussion of Hopkins, to summarize even a small portion of the now vast literature on textuality, discourse, and the dissemination of information.[1] Instead, I shall take as an exemplary characterization of the writer's relationship to his text in modern literary theory a passage from Edward Said's book *Beginnings*. The passage is especially pertinent to the present discussion since it is part of Said's superb interpretation of Hopkins:

> The central symbol for the modern producing writer depicts the physical transfer of an image from man's sexual-procreative life to his artistic one. A writer's writing, in other words, is the result of daring to apply sexual energy or attention to the act of writing. The image of the writer . . . is . . . an intensified confusion of production with product, of career with text, of textuality with sexuality, of image with career. The more a text is produced, the stronger (obviously) the temptation to regard sacrifices made for it, the arid and imageless technical logic of the career suffered for it, as gaining for the writer an overt libidinal gratification and in the long run offspring. The text's volume, its substantial textuality, collects not just the writer's writing, but also those energies, diverted from his sexual life, of procreative engenderment. . . . Both the words and the sexual energy are signs of the writer's activity: they are his product, his text and child.[2]

The sexual metaphor elucidated by Said has a special poignancy in the case of Hopkins, not only because of the celibate life he chose, but also because it is often in sexual imagery that Hopkins symbolizes his relationship to his own writing. Consider this quotation (cited some pages later by Said) from a letter to Canon Dixon dated June 30, 1886:

> Now this is the artist's most essential quality, masterly execution: it is a kind of male gift and especially marks off men from women, the begetting one's thought on paper, on verse, on whatever the matter is; the life must be conveyed into the work and be displayed there, not suggested as having been in the artist's mind. . . . Moreover on better consideration it strikes me that the mastery I speak of is not so much the male quality in the mind as a puberty in the life of that quality. The male quality is the creative gift. [L. II, 133]

Creativity is power, the will to power according to Nietzsche, the realization in a work of art of productive-procreative energies. The writer

---

[1]For a brief summary and synthesis of some of the current literature dealing with the problem of text and author, see Michael Sprinker, "Fictions of the Self," in *Autobiography*, ed. James Olney (Princeton: Princeton University Press, 1980).

[2]Edward W. Said, *Beginnings* (New York: Basic Books, 1975), pp. 263-64.

expends his vitality in the writing process, finding release for the pent-up
energy he possesses.

But Hopkins was equally aware of the negative side of the sexual
metaphor. The writer's sexual-creative power remains in a precarious
state. It can vanish suddenly, leaving the writer emasculated and impotent,
unable to accomplish more than the weak expression of a desire to
produce work. Less than a year before the letter to Dixon, Hopkins had
written to Bridges:

> An old question of yours I have hitehrto neglected to answer, am I
> thinking of writing on metre? I suppose thinking too much and doing
> too little. I do greatly desire to treat that subject; might perhaps get
> something together this year; but I can scarcely believe that on that
> or on anything else anything of mine will ever see the light—of
> publicity nor even of day. For it is widely true, the fine pleasure is not
> to do a thing but to feel that you could and the mortification that
> goes to the heart is to feel it is the power that fails you: *qui occidere
> nolunt Posse volunt;* it is the refusal of a thing that we like to have.
> So with me, if I could but get on, if I could but produce work I should
> not mind its being buried, silenced, and going no further; but it kills
> me to be time's eunuch and never to beget. [L. I, 221-22][3]

The writer (not merely the poet, for Hopkins refers here to a projected
work on meter) "begets" his text; textual production is a kind of procreation, the writer's texts his progeny. In his inability to write, Hopkins
experiences not only a loss of fecundity, but of all sexual energy and
power. It is not simply a question of publishing or not, though this
problem weighed on Hopkins as well, but of producing anything at all.
Unlike the Creator in "Pied Beauty" who "fathers-forth" the endless
variety of "dappled things" in the world, Hopkins is powerless to create,
to "father-forth," to write.

In the letters to Bridges of 1885, spiritual and intellectual impotence
assumes a physical form as well, as it did for many others (Conrad,
Flaubert, Coleridge, Faulkner, Dickens, Kafka, Proust, and Mallarmé
come immediately to mind as other celebrated examples). Hopkins is
"dying—of anaemia," "weak in body and harassed in mind," trapped "in
that coffin of weakness and dejection in which I live" (L. I, 208, 211,
214-15). Writing for him comes to demand a painful exertion of spirit

---

[3]The image is repeated in one of the last poems Hopkins wrote, less than six months
before his death: ". . . birds build—but not I build; no, but strain, / Time's eunuch, and not
breed one work that wakes" (P, 107).

and body: "I have after long silence written two sonnets, which I am touching: if ever anything was written in blood one of these was" (L. I, 219). Though Hopkins is certainly not alone among writers in having suffered physically from the activity of writing, he seems to have suffered greater incapacitation than most. His poetic output is, for a major poet, embarrassingly small. For Conrad, Faulkner, Dickens, Kafka, and Proust, physical anguish acted as a spur to further production;[4] in contrast, Hopkins's increasing physical debility was matched by a corresponding diminution in the quantity of his writing.

Hopkins, unlike other modern writers, attributes his suffering to his own sinfulness and to the will of God, and in his writing enacts a complex dialectic between willing and being enslaved to the will of another. Reading the spiritual meditations of the Dublin period, one is startled by the almost pathological conviction in Hopkins of personal responsibility for his spiritual state:

> The Incarnation was for my salvation and that of the world: the work goes on in a great system and machinery which even drags me on with the collar round my neck though I could and do neglect my duty in it. But I say to myself that I am only too willing to do God's work and help on the knowledge of the Incarnation. But this is not really true: I am not willing enough for the piece of work assigned me, the only work I am given to do, though I could do others if they were given. [S, 263][5]

He protests that he is "dragged" along by the will of God, but immediately he recognizes that his own will powerfully resists. He desires to make his own volition accord with the duty required of him, but he sees only too clearly that any act of personal will runs contrary to the divine purpose. This is the writer's central dilemma, to be pulled in opposite directions, on the one hand by his will to individuality and selfhood (the expression in writing of the desire to write), and on the other by the pressure of duty

[4]On disease as the central metaphor in and the driving force behind the writings of Proust and Kafka, see Walter Benjamin's essays on these two writers in *Illuminations*, ed. Hannah Arendt, trans. Harry Zohn (New York: Schocken Books, 1969). On the play of metaphor in Benjamin and Proust and on the way in which the written text produces the life rather than the other way around, see Carol Jacobs, *The Dissimulating Harmony* (Baltimore: Johns Hopkins University Press, 1978), pp. 89-110.

[5]Hopkins's recognition of a celestial "machinery which even drags me on with the collar round my neck" can be compared to the famous "knitting-machine" letter written by Joseph Conrad to his friend R. B. Cunninghame Graham (see *Joseph Conrad's Letters to R. B. Cunninghame Graham*, ed. C. T. Watts [Cambridge: At the University Press, 1969], pp. 56-57). The obvious pun on "collar" is familiar from the poem of that title by George Herbert.

(in Hopkins the duty to God, but in other writers to family, friends, society). Writing itself is the outcome of this conflict, though the text is frequently purchased at a frightful price, extracting ever more pain and requiring ever more exertion from the writer with each new stroke of the pen. The physical and mental strain of writing finally exhausts the writer's powers, so that he is capable of only the most feeble expressions of the desire to produce:

> I do not feel then that outwardly I do much good, much that I care to do or can much wish to prosper; and this is a mournful life to lead. In thought I can of course divide the good from the evil and live for the one, not the other: this justifies me but it does not alter the facts. Yet it seems to me that I could lead this life well enough if I had bodily energy and cheerful spirits. However these God will not give me. The other part, the more important, remains, my inward service. . . .
>
> I cannot then be excused; but what is life without aim, without spur, without help? All my undertakings miscarry: I am like a straining eunuch. I wish then for death: yet if I died now I should die imperfect, no master of myself, and that is the worst failure of all. O my God, look down on me. [S, 262][6]

The characteristic image of Hopkins's later career is that of a man lacking the sheer energy to produce anything at all except when compelled to do so against his will.[7]

---

[6]Father Devlin's note to this passage takes Hopkins to task for desiring more than is humanly possible: "There may be a symptomatic confusion of thought here. The state of perfection which the profession of a religious enjoins is a constant *striving* for perfection; the complete attainment of it is not possible in this life" (S, 319). This may be correct theology, but it scarcely does justice to the complexity of Hopkins's emotions. The desire for self-mastery is paradoxical in Hopkins, since it implies submission to God's will at the same time that it demands an assertion of personal will. As always in Hopkins, volition is not resolvable into good and evil components but carries the double sense of self-assertion and submission.

[7]Nor is this sense of his own failure confined to the privacy of his spiritual meditations. The letters to Bridges already cited show how Hopkins's experience of aridity, fatigue, and impotence found expression outside his private writings, as does the following passage from a letter to Baillie written April 24, 1885: "I think this is from a literary point of view (not from a moral) the worst letter I ever wrote to you, and it shall not run much longer. You will wonder I have been so long over it. This is part of my disease, so to call it. The melancholy I have all my life been subject to has become of late years not indeed more intense in its fits but rather more distributed, constant, and crippling. One, the lightest but a very inconvenient form of it, is daily anxiety about work to be done, which makes me break off or never finish all that lies outside that work. It is useless to write more on this: when I am at the worst, though my judgment is never affected, my state is much like madness. I see no ground for thinking I shall ever get over it or ever succeed in doing anything that is not forced on me to do of any consequence" (L. III, 256).

As many of Hopkins's commentators have noted, one of the crucial problems in reading his texts, and the cornerstone in many ways of his theory of poetry, is the concept of the self.[8] Hopkins identified writing with "selving" (his coinage of the verb form in "As kingfishers catch fire"); hence, selving is fundamental to the dialectic of willing and submission generated by Hopkins's writing. Late in life, Hopkins wrote to Bridges about his sense of himself as a writer:

> I *must* read something of Greek and Latin letters and lately I sent you a sonnet, on the Heraclitean Fire, in which a great deal of early Greek philosophical thought was distilled; but the liquor of the distillation did not taste very Greek, did it? The effect of studying masterpieces is to make me admire and do otherwise. So it must be on every original artist to some degree, on me to a marked degree. Perhaps then more reading would only *refine my singularity*, which is not what you want. [L. I, 291]

In a similar vein, Hopkins wrote to Patmore: "Every true poet, I thought, must be original and originality a condition of poetic genius; so that each poet is like a species in nature (*not* an *individuum genericum* or *specificum*) and can never recur" (L. III, 370).[9] The mark of the poet is his powerful individuality, his selfhood, which Hopkins attributed to volition. The writer creates himself, as a writer, by a special act of willing, through the agency of what Hopkins called the *arbitrium*:

> The tendency in the soul towards an infinite object comes from the *arbitrium*. The *arbitrium* in itself is man's personality or individuality and places him on a level of individuality in some sense with God; so that in so far as God is one thing, a self, an individual being, he is an object of apprehension, desire, pursuit to man's *arbitrium*. There

[8]See the excellent discussions of this theme in Hopkins's writings by Father Devlin in his introduction to part 2 of Hopkins's *Sermons and Devotional Writings* (S, 115-21), by J. Hillis Miller in *The Disappearance of God* (Cambridge: Harvard University Press, 1963), pp. 270-359, and by Edward W. Said in *Beginnings* (pp. 266-73).

[9]The point about species is of course thoroughly Darwinian; moreover, it accords with the common mid-nineteenth-century understanding of species as identifiable and isolable points in the grid of classification of biological creatures, centers of selfhood, one might say. Consider, for example, Ruskin's explanation in *The Queen of the Air*: "Species are not innumerable; neither are they now connected by consistent gradation. They touch at certain points only; and even then are connected, when we examine them deeply, in a kind of reticulated way, not in chains, but in chequers; also, however connected, it is but by a touch of the extremities, as it were, and the characteristic form of the species is entirely individual" (John Ruskin, *The Works of John Ruskin*, ed. E. T. Cook and Alexander Wedderburn, Library Ed., 39 vols. [London: G. Allen, 1903-1912], 19: 359).

would be no apprehension, desire, action, or motion of any kind
without freedom of play, that play which is given by the use of a
nature, of human nature, with its faculties; there would only be that
inchoate positive stress imperceptible in particular to itself; but with
the use of a nature and its faculties the strain of desire, pursuit, and
also consciousness of self begins. [S, 138-39]

The poet or writer wills to create, which is to say that the act of writing is
preeminently "selving," the achievement of individuality that puts the
writer "on a level of individuality in some sense with God." The self has
what Hopkins calls "freedom of pitch," "freedom of play," and "freedom
of field" (S, 147-49); it is what it is only by virtue of its power of conation.
Without volition, without freedom of play, the self is "indeed nothing, a
zero, in the score or account of existence" (S, 146).

The phrase "freedom of play" is particularly noteworthy in Hopkins's
imaging of the self, for it further illuminates the dialectic of willing and
submission at the source of this concept in Hopkins's thought. The self
would seem to be a kind of center, an origin, a univocal point from which
radiate all the qualities of the individual and all the works that he
produces. The self, in this formulation, is like a node of energy that
creates and sustains all the activities of an individual's being. One sees
why this concept of the self would suggest to Hopkins an analogy with
God, the *fons et origo* of all creation.[10] But the relationship of the self to
its productions is not so simple. Although no creation can occur without
the originating impulse of the self, the field of energy that it produces is
not a homogeneous dispersion structured by lines of force emanating
from the center. Each self is both self-originating and also conditioned;
each structure produced by the self is both centered in the self and
eccentric with respect to it, much as if a geometric figure could be a
circle and an ellipse at the same time, or, as in certain *Gestalt* diagrams,
one figure is in fact two figures neither of which can command the
attention of the viewer for more than a few moments. Hopkins's understanding of the self as nonunivocal is best illustrated by a long and
somewhat obscure passage in his fragmentary commentary on the
Spiritual Exercises of St. Ignatius. The passage illustrates how the concept

[10]Gerald Monsman, in "Pater, Hopkins, and the Self," *Victorian Newsletter* 46 (Fall
1974): 1-5, argues for the conceptualization of the self as center in Hopkins and Pater, both
of whom represent a continuation of the Platonic tradition of radical idealism. This view
ignores what one might call the atomistic strain in the writings of both Pater and Hopkins,
not to mention Plato himself, a tendency in their thought that generates the rather different
concept of the self I develop below.

of self as center breaks down for Hopkins under the force of its own implications. It is an exemplary moment in Hopkins's writing, because it discovers the essential eccentricity of the concept of selfhood in its own unfolding as a text. As a text, it enacts the very processes of decentering and deconstruction that it describes. Here is the passage:

> For, to speak generally, whatever can with truth be called a self . . . such as individuals and persons must be, it is not a mere centre or point of reference for consciousness or action attributed to it, everything else, all that it is conscious of or acts on being its object only and outside it. Part of this world of objects, this object-world, is also part of the very self in question, as in man's case his own body, which each man not only feels in and acts with but also feels and acts on. If the centre of reference spoken of has concentric circles round it, one of these, the inmost, say, is its own, is óf it, the rest are tó it only. Within a certain bounding line all will be self, outside of it nothing: with it self begins from one side and ends from the other. . . . A self then will consist of a centre *and* a surrounding area or circumference, of a point of reference *and* a belonging field, the latter set out, as surveyors etc say, from the former; of two elements, which we may call the inset and the outsetting or the display. Now this applies to the universal mind or being too; it will have its inset and its outsetting; only that the outsetting includes all things, with all of which it is in some way, by turns, in a series, or however it is, identified. But then this is an altogether different outsetting from what each of those very things to its own particular self has. And since self consists in the relation the inset and the outsetting bear to one another, the universal has a relation different from everything else and everything else from everything else, including the universal, so that the self of the universal is not the self of anything else. In other words the universal is not really identified with everything else nor with anything else, which was supposed; that is / there is no such universal. [S, 127]

Not the least notable feature of this passage is its tortured syntax, which can stand as a synecdoche for the twisting, shifting indecisiveness of Hopkins's textual practice. In prose, as in poetry, the syntactic labyrinth of Hopkins's style compels the reader to immerse himself completely in the text in order to decipher it. But as he intervenes, the reader discovers the tenuousness of his contact with the text itself, for it is all but impossible to reproduce (short of repeating the text verbatim—a technique of interpretation favored by Borges's Pierre Ménard) the text's cramped, repetitive, labored style. But this is, baldly and much too simply stated, the very point that the text itself labors mightily to make, to wit, that the self (read "text") cannot be reduced to "a mere centre or point of reference for consciousness or action attributed to it." The passage does not reproduce or represent this thought but *is* the thought produced on the page unfolding and folding back upon itself before the reader's attentive gaze.

The passage opens with an apparently unequivocal assertion about the self, that it is not "a mere centre or point of reference." It then reverses itself and presents the self as the center of a series of concentric circles, some (perhaps only one) of which are bound to the central point of the self, others being merely related, in some inexplicable way, to the self. But in what way is this outside related to the self if not as part of it? Can the self be both separate from the concentric circles around it and at the same time "consist of a centre *and* a surrounding area or circumference, of a point of reference *and* a belonging field"? What is the precise relationship of this center to the field that circumscribes it and is, one presumes (what else can the concept of a center signify?), structurally or topographically defined by the center? The passage does not resolve this question but turns away from it (while commenting upon it in an oblique manner) to consider the meaning of "the universal mind or being," a topic treated in a subsequent paragraph with direct reference to God. Can the universal be a self properly speaking? The text says so but immediately rejects what it has proposed, annulling the concept of the universal self which is revealed to be a contradiction in terms: "The universal is not really identified with everything else nor with anything else, which was supposed; that is / there is no such universal." But already, in the very formulation of the concept of the self, this contradiction has appeared. Though the universal self would be logically and ontologically prior to any particular self, even to the concept of selfhood, no such concept as the universal self can be sustained in the face of the already insupportable contradictions presented by the description of the self. The text struggles to produce or even to describe what such a concept as the universal self might be, but it fails to achieve any satisfactory description of the universal in relation to the field that it produces: "[the universal mind or being] will have its inset and its outsetting; only that the outsetting includes all things, with all of which it is in some way, by turns, in a series, or however it is, identified." Just as the relationship of the self to its surrounding field is never resolved in the text, so the relationship of the universal to other things remains undecidable, including "all things," identified with them, but only "in some way, by turns, in a series, or however it is." The despairing conclusion of the text, that "there is no such universal," partially conceals but cannot entirely avoid the silent but inevitable conclusion of the text's inexorable logic: there is no such self either. The text says this without saying it, means it without intending it, reaches its conclusion by willing to do otherwise. In the end, all that the text can accomplish is its own production; all that Hopkins can accomplish is the production of the text. The self that authors this writing is no more responsible for, no more in control of, no more the center or origin of the writing than any self is the center or origin of anything outside itself. For Hopkins, the composition of a text on the concept of the self reveals the ineluctable textuality of selfhood. The self is nothing more than the text recorded on the page and preserved in the book.

If the self as authoring principle is radically textual, then certain of Hopkins's statements about his own writing appear less strange and aberrant. For example, Hopkins wrote to Bridges apropos of the "terrible sonnets" composed late in his life: "Four of these [sonnets] came like inspirations unbidden and against my will. And in the life I lead now, which is one of a continually jaded and harassed mind, if in any leisure I try to do anything I make no way—nor with my work, alas! but so it must be" (L. I, 221). The profession of an inability to produce, the realiza-tion of texts without any overt act of willing, the text of the letter itself witnessing both the suffering of the writer and his continuing capacity to write—these familiar landmarks in Hopkins's work are not momentary or eccentric but are, rather, signs of the regular textual practice evident in all of his writings. Writing expresses the ceaseless dialectic between willing and submission that Hopkins again and again recognizes as the special destiny of the self in the world. Writing is preeminently "selving," a conative act circumscribed by the opposing pressure of other selves, of the world, and ultimately of God.

That the notion of selving had for Hopkins the most far-reaching significance is undeniable. It bears not only upon the theory of poetry that was ceaselessly evolving throughout his career, but upon the most crucial problems of theology and the spiritual life as well. Most clearly in his devotional writings, Hopkins lays bare the immense importance of selving to his spiritual life. During the retreat he made in November 1881, he meditated intensely upon the mysteries of creation, redemption, and Christ's sacrifice. In the writings of this period, the concept of selving is powerfully evoked in the figures of Christ and Lucifer. Christ's Incarnation and His sacrifice provide Hopkins with the perfect exemplar of selving:

This sacrifice and this outward procession is a consequence and shadow of the procession of the Trinity, from which mystery sacrifice takes its rise. . . . It is as if the blissful agony or stress of selving in God had forced out drops of sweat or blood, which drops were the world, or as if the lights lit at the festival of the "peaceful Trinity" through some little cranny striking out lit up into being one "cleave" out of the world of possible creatures. The sacrifice would be the Eucharist, and that the victim might be truly victim like, like motionless, helpless, or lifeless, it must be in matter. [S, 197]

The passage summarizes the Scotist doctrine of the Incarnation. According to Scotus, the Incarnation was before time, while Christ's entry into the world as a man and his death on the cross were a consequence of the Fall. As Father Devlin points out: "It is like distinguishing two events in the great sentence of St. John: 'The Word was made flesh—and came to dwell among us'" (S, 114).[11] For Hopkins, Christ is the preeminent example of the self "pitched" toward God, the perfect embodiment of what he elsewhere calls the "affective will" (S, 149). Hopkins is completely orthodox in his opinion that the fullest realization of self is Christ's Sacrifice and that the finite selves in the world strive toward this state of harmony with divine purpose. Where Hopkins departs from orthodoxy, however, is in the contrary and equal emphasis he places upon Lucifer as exemplar of the *arbitrium*, or elective will.[12]

Hopkins's meditations on the figure of Lucifer are among the most interesting passages in his devotional writings. In the Christian tradition, Lucifer is the great opponent of Christ, and Hopkins is thus entirely conventional in contrasting the two as representatives of sin and obedi-

---

[11]Father Devlin's explanation of Hopkins's "Scotism" (S, 108-15) is the best introduction to this complex topic. To illustrate Hopkins's understanding of the Incarnation, he quotes the following passage from Scotus's *Scriptum Oxoniense*: "I say then, but without insisting on it, that before the Incarnation and 'before Abraham was,' in the beginning of the world, Christ could have had a true temporal existence in a sacramental manner. And if this is true, it follows that before the conception and formation of the Body of Christ from the most pure blood of the Glorious Virgin there could have been the Eucharist" (S, 113-14).

[12]Father Devlin discusses the distinction between elective will and affective will (which he labels "desire" and "choice" respectively) and questions "whether Hopkins was right in sometimes taking for granted an inevitable opposition between the two" (S, 116). He finds a particularly disturbing instance of the separation of desire from choice in the image of the soul "wrestling with God" in the final line of "Carrion Comfort": "It is an image which is somehow alien to Catholic spirituality" (S, 118). It is not, however, an image alien to the spirit of Hopkins.

ence. But the terms he employs to characterize the sin of Lucifer are startling:

> This song of Lucifer's was a dwelling on his own beauty, an instressing of his own inscape, and like a performance on the organ and instrument of his own being; it was a sounding, as they say, of his own trumpet and a hymn in his own praise. Moreover it became an incantation: others were drawn in; it became a concert of voices, a concerting of selfpraise, an enchantment, a magic, by which they were dizzied, dazzled, and bewitched. They would not listen to the note which summoned each to his own place (Jude 6.) and distributed them here and there in the liturgy of the sacrifice; they gathered rather closer and closer home under Lucifer's lead and drowned it, raising a countermusic and countertemple and altar, a counterpoint of dissonance and not of harmony. [S, 200-201]

The passage has an intense poignancy for Hopkins, for his own aim in poetry was to achieve "an instressing of his own inscape." The image of Lucifer's rebellion as a "countermusic," a "counterpoint of dissonance," reproduces the metaphors Hopkins often employed to characterize his own poetic activity. Lucifer's song is precisely that species of unnatural music which Hopkins perpetually claimed he himself created. Recall the letter to Bridges in which Hopkins defends the "oddness" of his poetry: "No doubt my poetry errs on the side of oddness. . . . But as air, melody, is what strikes me most of all in music and design in painting, so design, pattern or what I am in the habit of calling 'inscape' is what I above all aim at in poetry. Now it is the virtue of design, pattern, or inscape to be distinctive and it is the vice of distinctiveness to become queer. This vice I cannot have escaped" (L. I, 66). Hopkins's poetry strives to maintain a precarious balance between virtue and vice, between harmony and dissonance, between the proper praise of God and the "concerting of self-praise." The career of the religious poet remained forever in the shadow of the disobedient sinner.[13]

[13]Much has been written about the conflict in Hopkins between his duty as a priest and his desire to write poetry. The tension he felt is evident in a letter to Canon Dixon written November 11, 1881, in which Hopkins responds to Dixon's wish to have some of Hopkins's poetry published: "My vocation puts before me a standard so high that a higher can be found nowhere else. The question then for me is not whether I am willing . . . to make a sacrifice of hopes of fame (let us suppose), but whether I am not to undergo a severe judgment from God for the lothness I have shewn in making it, for the reserves I may have in my heart made, for the backward glances I have given with my hand upon the plough, for the waste of time the very compositions you admire may have caused and their preoccupation of the mind which belonged to more sacred or more binding duties, for the disquiet and the thoughts of vainglory they have given rise to" (L. II, 88). The question of

The archetype of the disobedient sinner, and hence of the poet as well, is Lucifer. Lucifer possessed a special fascination for Hopkins (as he did for Milton), not only as the adversary of Christ, but in the curious blend of beauty and corruption that he exemplified. This fascination is illuminated by a remarkable passage on the iconography of the devil as serpent or dragon. It is an important moment not only in Hopkins's writings but in the intellectual history of the nineteenth century as well, for it has significant analogues in passages from Pater and Ruskin (and later in Yeats) and thus forms a node or point of convergence for certain motifs in nineteenth-century aesthetics. Here is the passage from Hopkins:

> A coil or spiral is then a type of the Devil, who is called the old (or original) serpent, and this I suppose because of its "swale" or subtle and imperceptible drawing in towards its head or centre, and it is a type of death, of motion lessening and at last ceasing. *Invidia autem diaboli mors intravit in mundum:* God gave things a forward and perpetual motion; the Devil, that is / thrower of things off the track, upsetter, mischiefmaker, clashing one with another brought in the law of decay and consumption in inanimate nature, death in the vegetable and animal world, moral death and original sin in the world of man. . . .
>
> The snake or serpent a symbol of the Devil. So also the Dragon. . . . So that if the Devil is symbolised as a snake he must be an arch-snake and a dragon. Mostly dragons are represented as much more than serpents, but always as in some way reptiles. Now among the vertebrates the reptiles go near to combine the qualities of the other classes in themselves and are, I think, taken by the Evolutionists as nearest the original vertebrate stem and as the point of departure for the rest. In this way clearly dragons are represented as gathering up the attributes of many creatures: they are reptiles always, but besides sometimes have bat's wings; four legs, sometimes those of the mammal quadrupeds, sometimes birds' feet and talons; jaws some-times of crocodiles, but sometimes of eagles; armouring like crocodiles again, but also sturgeons and other fish, or lobsters and other crustacea; or like insects; colours like the dragonfly and other insects; sometimes horns; and so on. And therefore I suppose the dragon as a type of the Devil to express the universality of his powers, both the gifts he has by nature and the attributes and sway he grasps, and the

---

whether or not to publish his poetry did not trouble Hopkins so much as the very fact of his desire to write poetry at all. Writing continued to pose a temptation for Hopkins throughout his career, and he consistently opposed his will to write to his duty to God and the Jesuit order.

horror which the whole inspires. . . . The dragon then symbolises one who aiming at every perfection ends by being a monster, a "fright." [S, 198-99]

This might have been written by a Renaissance mythographer, or perhaps taken from a book of emblems.[14] Hopkins writes in the vein of an allegorist illuminating the "dark conceits" of Christian iconography—and what a brilliant and original piece of *allegoresis* it is!

Hopkins, like Dante, images perfection in the form of a circle. "God gave things a forward and perpetual motion"—presumably in the form of a perfect circle. Satan upsets this perfect motion, bringing death into the world and causing the motion of creation to fall into a decaying spiral. The image of the spiral or coil also suggests to Hopkins the serpent as an emblem for the Devil (see Genesis 3: 15), presumably because of the habit of snakes to lie coiled when at rest, but also because of the numerous iconographic representations of Satan in the form of a serpent coiled around the Tree of Knowledge tempting Adam and Eve to Original Sin. These two emblems reinforce each other; the image of the spiral harmonizes with the image of the serpent. But the serpent is also a dragon, a much more complicated emblem. As Hopkins knew, dragons are mythical beasts, resembling serpents (or worms, as they are often called in Anglo-Saxon literature), but having frequently as well the attributes of fish, crocodiles, crustacea, eagles, bats, and insects. The dragon is a composite creature (as "the Cherubim are in Scripture," Hopkins notes) with numerous attributes that can vary from representation to representation. The dragon is a serpent and yet more than a serpent, but always in some way reptilean. Reptiles themselves are, in the chain of vertebrates, very close to being "the original vertebrate stem," hence partakers in the attributes of all the rest. Thus serpents are in themselves a particular species of creature and also the figurative embodiment of all other vertebrates that descend from them. Just as Satan is the origin of evil and death and of the departure of the motion of creation from its perfectly circular path, so the serpent is the original of all vertebrate creatures, including man. And yet at the same time, neither Satan nor the serpent is truly original, for the motion of creation originates in God, and vertebrates are preceded in the evolutionary chain by invertebrates. The

[14]The similarity in style between Hopkins's poetry and seventeenth-century art and emblem books is suggested by Alan Heuser, *The Shaping Vision of Gerard Manley Hopkins* (London: Oxford University Press, 1958), pp. 96-97, 117-18. Heuser believes that Jesuit influence on the art of the Counter-Reformation links Hopkins's intellectual milieu to that of the seventeenth century.

serpent seems to be the point of convergence between vertebrate and invertebrate, just as Satan, in the figure of the dragon, embodies the convergence of beauty and corruption. He "symbolises one who aiming at every perfection ends by being a monster, a 'fright.'" Satan, the serpent, the dragon—all are emblems that cannot be resolved into univocal meanings, original figures which under examination reveal their difference from genuine originality. They are allegorical signs whose value or signification is a function of their relation to other signs in the system of the allegory. Satan is serpent and dragon; dragons are serpents and a host of other creatures; serpents partake of the nature of vertebrates and invertebrates—all are both beautiful and monstrous, strangely attractive and yet frightful.

This irresolvable doubleness is present already in the first figure mentioned by Hopkins, the spiral, a classical image for the simultaneity of rectilinear and circular motion.[15] The passage itself is a kind of spiral, moving from the central image of Satan as serpent toward a vague conception of the dragon as a composite of many creatures, then recoiling upon itself to repeat twice the controlling idea of the whole, the horror and fright inspired by Satan. Hopkins's prose coils and uncoils, producing in the text the very patterns of deviation from simplicity that are equated with the motion initiated by Satan in creation. Hopkins's writing is an emblem of his own troubled sense of what it means to write; his style achieves the frightful beauty he associates with Lucifer. And just as Lucifer's assertion of self-will, his "instressing of his own inscape," forced the circular motion of creation to deviate into a downward spiral, so the instressing of the inscape in the poet, the exercise of his *arbitrium* in writing, creates the strain of writing and living characteristic of Hopkins's later career. As Hopkins's career progressed, his writing became a "subtle and imperceptible drawing in towards its head or centre." His texts tended more and more toward entropy, toward "motion lessening and at last ceasing."

Hopkins's fascination with Lucifer as a figure for the duality of the artist marks an important moment in the history of Romantic aesthetics.

[15]See John Freccero, "Donne's 'Valediction Forbidding Mourning,'" *ELH* 30 (1963): 341. Freccero quotes from Chalcidius's commentary on the *Timaeus* to illustrate the significance of the spiral as a figure for the human approximation of the perfect circular motion of God, showing how the image of the compass and the spiral figure it creates is a commonplace in Renaissance emblem books. For a sweeping interpretation of the transformations undergone by the figure of the circle in European literature and philosophy since the Middle Ages, see Georges Poulet, *The Metamorphoses of the Circle*, trans. Carley Dawson and Elliott Coleman (Baltimore: Johns Hopkins University Press, 1966).

It points in two directions at once: forward in time toward the *fin de siècle* aestheticism which was in part the legacy of Hopkins's tutor Walter Pater and Pater's disciple W. B. Yeats, and backward toward traditional techniques of allegorical representation which remained alive in the middle decades of the nineteenth century primarily in the work of John Ruskin. The figure of Lucifer as serpent or dragon embodying the very type of corrupted beauty has its counterpart in a passage from Pater's essay on Leonardo Da Vinci in *The Rennaissance* in which Pater describes Leonardo's portrait of the *Medusa* that hangs in the Uffizi in Florence:

> The subject [of the Medusa] has been treated in various ways; Leonardo alone cuts to its centre; he alone realises it as the head of a corpse, exercising its powers through all the circumstances of death. What may be called the fascination of corruption penetrates in every touch its exquisitely finished beauty. About the dainty lines of the cheek the bat flits unheeded. The delicate snakes seem literally strangling each other in terrified struggle to escape from the Medusa brain. The hue which violent death always brings with it is in the features; features singularly massive and grand, as we catch them inverted, in a dexterous foreshortening, crown foremost, like a great calm stone against which the wave of serpents breaks.[16]

Beauty that is somehow disquieting, "so exotic that it fascinates a larger number than it delights,"[17] is the dominant motif in Pater's portrait of Leonardo. Its most famous expression comes in the description of *La Gioconda*, who possesses "a beauty wrought out from within upon the flesh, the deposit, little cell by cell, of strange thoughts and fantastic reveries and exquisite passions," a beauty "into which the soul with all its maladies has passed!"[18] Leonardo is for Pater the preeminently modern artist whose work retains "a certain mystery," "something enigmatical beyond the usual measure of great men"; he at once "fascinates, or perhaps half repels."[19] Just as Leonardo himself was fascinated by corrup-

[16]Walter Pater, *The Renaissance* (1873; rpt. London: Macmillan, 1922), p. 106. On Pater's affiliation with the aestheticism of the later nineteenth century and his decisive impact on the aesthetic thought of the twentieth century, see J. Hillis Miller, "Walter Pater," *Daedalus* 105 (Winter 1976): 97-113. Pater's idea of "the fascination of corruption" lies behind much of Yeats's aesthetics, of course, including the image of Satan in Yeats's celebration of Byzantium in *A Vision:* "This vision, this proclamation of their invisible master, had the Greek nobility, Satan always the still half-divine Serpent, never the horned scarecrow of the didactic Middle Ages" (W. B. Yeats, *A Vision* [1938; rpt. New York: Macmillan, 1956], p. 280).
[17]Pater, *The Renaissance*, p. 99.
[18]Ibid., p. 125.
[19]Ibid., p. 98.

tion and beauty in the *Medusa*, so Pater is transfixed by the image of Leonardo as both fascinating and repellant, like the "delicate snakes" which are "literally strangling each other in terrified struggle to escape from the Medusa brain."

Nowhere does Pater directly relate the serpents in the Medusa head of Leonardo to the serpent as allegorical sign for the Devil. This connection is made, obliquely to be sure, in another seminal text of the mid-nineteenth century, the fifth volume of Ruskin's *Modern Painters*, a text that both Pater and Hopkins must surely have known.[20] In his allegorical interpretation of Turner's *Garden of Hesperides*, Ruskin traces the lineage of the Hesperides' dragon (on the authority of Hesiod) to Phorcys and Ceto, two of the offspring of Nereus from whose incestuous union issued the dragon and also the Gorgons. Ruskin continues his account of the dragon's heritage and makes the somewhat startling connection between this figure in Greek mythology and the serpent of Genesis:

> But, in its moral significance, the descent is this. Covetousness, or malignity (Phorcys), and Secretness (Ceto), beget, first, the darkening passions, whose hair is always gray; then the stormy and merciless passions, brazen-winged (the Gorgons), of whom the dominant, Medusa, is ice-cold, turning all who look on her to stone. And, lastly, the consuming (poisonous and volcanic) passions—the "flame-backed dragon," uniting the powers of poison, and instant destruction. Now the reader may have heard, perhaps, in other books of Genesis than Hesiod's, of a dragon being busy about a tree which bore apples, and of crushing the head of that dragon; but seeing how, in the Greek mind, this serpent was descended from the sea, he may perhaps, be surprised to remember another verse, bearing also on the matter: —"Thou brakest the heads of the dragons in the waters"; and yet more surprising, going on with the Septuagint version, to find where he is being led: "Thou brakest the head of the dragon, and gavest him to be meat to the Ethiopian people. Thou didst tear asunder the strong fountains and the storm-torrents; thou didst dry up the rivers of Etham."[21]

The dragon and the Medusa represent opposite attributes of nature, volcanic fire and atmospheric cold respectively. In another place, Ruskin

---

[20] Hopkins quotes, somewhat incorrectly, from volume four of *Modern Painters* in a journal entry for September 14, 1871 (J, 215). His general acquaintance with Ruskin's works is evident from frequent references to Ruskin's opinions in his letters (L. II, 52, 131, 135; L. III, 202, 203-4, 313-14).

[21] Ruskin, *Works*, 7: 397-98.

remarks that the head of Medusa "signifies, I believe, the cloudy coldness of knowledge, and its venomous character."[22] And several paragraphs after the one quoted above, he identifies the Hesperian dragon with "the 'Pluto il gran nemico' of Dante; the demon of all evil passions connected with covetousness; that is to say, essentially a fraud, rage, and gloom."[23] Though the two figures signify quite different moral qualities, they share the common attributes of the serpent whose bite is death. Ruskin also complicates the story of the Hesperian dragon by introducing a different tradition about its descent, one in which the dragon is the grandchild of Medusa by Echidna, "half-maiden, half-serpent," a figure for treachery allegorically related, Ruskin says, to Judas's betrayal of Christ in Gethsemane. In Ruskin's recapitulation and interpretation of the myth, the Hesperian dragon, the Medusa, and the figure of the serpent insinuate themselves again and again in Christian iconography in episodes involving sin, betrayal, and death. Like Hopkins, Ruskin finds in the figure of the dragon-serpent the perfect embodiment of the adversary of virtue.

The dragon-serpent is a forbidding figure in Turner's painting, but Ruskin elsewhere expands upon the meaning of the serpent and shows how it also suggests the exact opposite of the horror inspired by the Hesperian dragon. In *The Queen of the Air*, Ruskin discusses the mythic significance of the serpent, apropos of the aegis of Athena which bears the image of the head of Medusa with its tangle of serpents. Of the serpent, Ruskin says: "It is a divine hieroglyph of the demoniac power of the earth,—of the entire earthly nature. As the bird is the clothed power of the air, so this is the clothed power of the dust; as the bird the symbol of the spirit of life, so this of the grasp and sting of death."[24] But this interpretation is incomplete, for, as Ruskin notes, the serpent is also a figure for the spirit of healing (associated with Aesculapius and Hygieia) and of wisdom (figured in the killing of the Python at Delphi which empowers the oracle that continues to reside there). Ruskin emphasizes the inherent duality of the serpent as allegorical sign, arguing that it embodies the spirit of beauty and the spirit of corruption and disease at the same time. All religions, he claims, exhibit this double spirit, even Christianity:

> In the Psalter of S. Louis itself, half of its letters are twisted snakes; there is scarcely a wreathed ornament, employed in Christian dress,

22 Ibid., 7: 184.
23 Ibid., 7: 400-401.
24 Ibid., 19: 363.

or architecture, which cannot be traced back to the serpent's coil; and there is rarely a piece of monkish decorated writing in the world, that is not tainted with some ill-meant vileness of grotesque. . . . And truly, it seems to me, as I gather in my mind the evidences of insane religion, degraded art, merciless war, sullen toil, detestable pleasure, and vain or vile hope, in which the nations of the world have lived since first they could bear record of themselves—it seems to me, I say, as if the race itself were still half-serpent, not extricated yet from its clay; a lacertine breed of bitterness—the glory of it emaciate [sic] with cruel hunger, and blotted with venomous stain: and the track of it, on the leaf a glittering slime, and in the sand a useless furrow.[25]

Ruskin's tracing of the mythological lineage of the serpent illuminates and enriches Hopkins's interpretation of the serpentine qualities of Lucifer. The image of the serpent as archetype of corrupted beauty, according to Ruskin, has a wide currency among the religious traditions of the world. The human fascination with serpents is a sign of the corrupted nature of man, "as if the race itself were still half-serpent, not extricated yet from its clay." Like the head of the Medusa painted by Leonardo, intensely beautiful and yet horrifying at the same time, the serpent is a figure for an irreducible contradiction in human nature. Its beauty is always blended with decadence and disease, with a sense of horror and the grotesque. This is the beauty that fascinated Hopkins in Lucifer; it is the destructive beauty of the poet, the sign of the writer's vocation which Hopkins both feared and desired.

The beautiful and the grotesque, fear and desire, willing and submission, sublime excess and painful *askesis*—these are the dominant themes of Hopkins's poetry, as they are the persistent tensions in his career as a poet. For Hopkins, poetry was the act of producing the self, one version of that selving which he associated not only with Christ but with Lucifer. To be a poet, for Hopkins and for other major writers, was to create a personal style, to become oneself in the act of writing by differentiating one's writing from the stylistic heritage of others. But the queerness and oddness of Hopkins's style was for him both a virtue and a vice, both beautiful and grotesque, "barbarous in beauty" (P, 70), as he says in a famous lyric. The drama of his career and the energy of his poetry is sustained by the conflict between these inseparable and irreconcilable aspects of his style.

[25]Ibid., 19: 365.

IV THE ELEGIAC SUBLIME
AND THE BIRTH OF THE POET:
"THE WRECK OF
THE DEUTSCHLAND"

The breath whose might I have invoked in song
Descends on me; my spirit's bark is driven
Far from the shore, far from the trembling throng
Whose sails were never to the tempest given;
The massy earth and spherèd skies are riven!
I am borne darkly, fearfully, afar;
Whilst, burning through the inmost veil of Heaven,
The soul of Adonais, like a star,
Beacons from the abode where the Eternal are.

—*Shelley*, "Adonais"

TRADITION HAS ESTABLISHED "The Wreck of the Deutschland" as the first great poem of Hopkins's maturity. At the same time, tradition has canonized the poem's difficulty and obscurity, its resistance to interpretation. On this as on so many points in Hopkins, Robert Bridges is most acute:

> The labour spent on this great metrical experiment must have served to establish the poet's prosody and perhaps his diction: therefore the poem stands logically as well as chronologically in the front of his book, like a great dragon folded in the gate to forbid all entrance, and confident in his strength from past success. This editor advises the reader to circumvent him and attack him later in the rear; for he was himself shamefully worsted in a brave frontal assault, the more easily perhaps because both subject and treatment were distasteful to him.[1]

Bridges's metaphor for the poem, repeated by subsequent critics, has become as much a part of our image of Hopkins's poetry as Hopkins's

---

[1]Robert Bridges, Preface to *Poems of Gerard Manley Hopkins*, ed. Robert Bridges, 2nd ed. (London: Oxford University Press, 1930), p. 104.

own figures. But few commentators have realized the extraordinary insight of Bridges into the constitutive role of "The Wreck of the Deutschland" in Hopkins's career as a poet. Bridges is most perceptive in recognizing that the poem was a great labor, that it was a "metrical experiment," and that it "served to establish the poet's prosody and perhaps his diction." In short, "The Wreck of the Deutschland" marked Hopkins's realization of a personal poetic style, his birth into a mature, strong poetry. Bridges is even more acute to discern how Hopkins, in giving birth to himself as a poet, achieved a forbidding strength that repulses the weak interpretive strategies of later readers. As if in anticipation of Harold Bloom, Bridges represents the act of reading as a romantic quest, a relationship of power and struggle between reader and poem. The dragon that lies "folded in the gate to forbid all entrance" to Hopkins's treasure hoard of verse is preternaturally strong, growing stronger with each new effort to overcome him. But whence comes this dragon's imposing strength? Why is this poem so difficult?

Bridges's complaints about Hopkins's faults of style, his "oddity and obscurity," have often been cited as examples of his failure to comprehend or to sympathize with his friend's verbal and rhythmic distinction. It has become almost obligatory among Hopkins's commentators to excoriate Bridges for his critical short-sightedness, his inability to understand the depths and intensities of Hopkins's religious feelings, and his finicky sense of stylistic propriety. The effort has been made to naturalize Hopkins, to "canonize" him (the very word used by F. R. Leavis in the opening sentence of his 1944 *Scrutiny* essay), to question and minimize the force of Bridges's metaphor. But the power of Bridges's insight remains, for "The Wreck of the Deutschland" *is* a difficult poem, it *is* rhythmically innovative and unusual, its diction, its rhymes, and its figures *are* often complex to the point of obscurity, and it does offend our sense of literary decorum. "The Wreck of the Deutschland" is one of the most indecorous poems in the language; it is also one of the greatest, not a little due to its studied and willful breaches of decorum. Bridges was certainly correct to note the oddity and obscurity of Hopkins's verse; he erred only in judging these qualities inexcusable faults. Like Shakespeare's Prince Hal, Hopkins's poems do "so offend to make offense a skill / Redeeming time when men think least [they] will." The redemption of time in sprung rhythm may be Hopkins's saving grace as a poet; it is undoubtedly the central discovery that gave birth to his poetic style.

Hopkins's own account of the genesis of "The Wreck of the Deutschland" establishes the poem as the crucial moment in his poetic career, the moment when he achieved the distinctive individuality of style which he prized so highly and which every poet struggles toward. Hopkins saw quite clearly what all of his commentators since Bridges have also seen, that "The Wreck of the Deutschland" was his first major poem, the first distinctive verse in a style truly Hopkinsian. His seven years of poetic silence were not only an expression of devotion to his religious vocation but a confession of the weakness of his early verse. Written in the shadow of Keats and Tennyson, Hopkins's early poems possess none of the originality, the virtuosity, the sheer power that emerge in "The Wreck of the Deutschland." Hopkins's account of the poem's origins comes in a letter to Canon Dixon written in October 1878, nearly three years after the poem's composition and in the wake of the remarkable creative burst that succeeded it and produced the nature sonnets of 1877. Here is Hopkins's self-analysis:

> You ask, do I write verse myself. What I had written I burnt before I became a Jesuit and resolved to write no more, as not belonging to my profession, unless it were by the wish of my superiors; so for seven years I wrote nothing but two or three little presentation pieces which occasion called for. But when in the winter of '75 the Deutsch-land was wrecked in the mouth of the Thames and five Franciscan nuns, exiles from Germany by the Falck Laws, aboard of her were drowned I was affected by the account and happening to say so to my rector he said that he wished someone would write a poem on the subject. On this hint I set to work and, though my hand was out at first, produced one. I had long had haunting my ear the echo of a new rhythm which now I realised on paper. To speak shortly, it consists in scanning by accents or stresses alone, without any account of the number of syllables, so that a foot may be one strong syllable or it may be many light and one strong. I do not say the idea is altogether new; there are hints of it in music, in nursery rhymes and popular jingles, in the poets themselves, and, since then, I have seen it talked about as a thing possible in critics. . . . But no one has pro-fessedly used it and made it the principle throughout, that I know of. Nevertheless to me it appears, I own, to be a better and more natural principle than the ordinary system, much more flexible, and capable of much greater effects. However I had to mark the stresses in blue chalk, and this and my rhymes carried on from one line into another and certain chimes suggested by the Welsh poetry I had been reading (what they call *cynghanedd*) and a great many more oddnesses could

not but dismay an editor's eye, so that when I offered it to our magazine the *Month*, though at first they accepted it, after a time they withdrew and dared not print it. After writing this I held myself free to compose, but cannot find it in my conscience to spend time upon it; so I have done little and shall do less. [L. II, 14-15]

"The Wreck of the Deutschland" represented an equivocal achievement for Hopkins. On the one hand, he recognized and valued highly his discovery of sprung rhythm ("no one has professedly used it and made it the principle throughout"), but on the other he saw all too clearly the difficulty that this rhythm and the attendant liberties ("a great many more oddnesses") in rhyme, diction, and grammar would present to the average reader. At one point, Hopkins even felt he ought to give the reader elaborate instructions about the metrical structure of the poem and appended a note on the scansion to one of the autographs he sent to Bridges (see P, 255-56). To some extent, Hopkins sympathized with the decision of the editor of the *Month* not to publish the poem, though he was at the same time dismayed to think that his poetry was so extravagant and idiosyncratic as to be beyond understanding. Nevertheless, the stylistic innovations of "The Wreck of the Deutschland" were to enable all of Hopkins's subsequent poetry. Sprung rhythm, often with the stresses marked to aid the reader, "rhymes carried on from one line into another," "certain chimes suggested by Welsh poetry," "and a great many more oddnesses"—these were to remain the distinctive features of Hopkins's poetic style, though he became more and more distressed by the reaction of his readers (principally Dixon and Bridges, though later Coventry Patmore as well), who found his poems difficult and obscure. Hopkins's ambivalence towards his special achievement as a poet is evident in the last sentence quoted from the letter to Dixon: "After writing this I held myself free to compose, but cannot find it in my conscience to spend time upon it; so I have done little and shall do less." During the ten years of life that remained to him, Hopkins was never again to experience the burst of creative energy that produced "The Wreck of the Deutschland" and the nature sonnets composed slightly more than a year after it. The arc of Hopkins's career is a curve of diminishing magnitude, originating in the celebrations of poetic birth and creativity in the sublime mode of "The Wreck of the Deutschland," descending to the curtailed sublimity of the nature sonnets (of which "The Windhover" and "Pied Beauty" are the best examples), culminating in the severe *askesis* of the late poems which depict the ebbing and ultimate loss of the poet's creative power. This is why "The Wreck of the Deutschland" is such an equivocal achievement. For the rest of his life, Hopkins stood in awe of the grandeur of this poem, desiring once again to attain the Sublime, but knowing that he was incapable of doing so. Though "The Wreck of the Deutschland" left him "free to compose," at the same time its great poetic strength and originality inhibited each subsequent composition. The poem registers an extra-ordinary gain (the birth of the poet in the creation of a personal style) but also a poignant loss (of the self whose life did not require the severe *askesis* portrayed in "The Wreck of the Deutschland"). Hopkins was understandably ambivalent about the achievement of the poem, for it represented an ideal (of poetic style and of spiritual life) that was all but impossible to sustain. The burden of this ideal weighed heavily on all the poetry he was to write.

That "The Wreck of the Deutschland" is an autobiographical poem about the birth of the poet can be shown from evidence within and outside the poem. The letter to Dixon establishes the centrality of the poem to Hopkins's attainment of a personal poetic style, and a letter to Bridges written approximately eight months prior to the letter to Dixon makes clear the poem's autobiographical aspects: "I may add for your greater interest and edification that what refers to myself in the poem is all strictly and literally true and did all occur; nothing is added for poetical padding" (L. I, 47). W. H. Gardner cites this remark in reference to the poem's second stanza (see P, 257), which seems to be an account of Hopkins's conversion experience. But there are numerous other references to the self of the poet throughout the poem, many of which deal directly with the poet's relationship to the tall nun who is the poem's heroine. For example, in stanza eighteen Hopkins exclaims:

> Ah, touched in your bower of bone,
> Are you! turned for an exquisite smart,
> Have you! make words break from me here all alone,
> Do you!—mother of being in me, heart.
> O unteachably after evil, but uttering truth,
> Why, tears! is it? tears; such a melting, a madrigal start!
> Never-eldering revel and river of youth,
> What can it be, this glee? the good you have there of your own?

The suffering of the tall nun, and later, her summoning Christ to her, the cry "O Christ, Christ, come quickly," recalls to the poet the memory of his own similar moment of confrontation with the divine, represented throughout the first ten stanzas of the poem, but most directly invoked in stanza two. The nun's suffering calls forth the voice of the poet. Hopkins is directly touched, in his heart, he says, by the image of the nun; his voice arises at the bidding of her exclamation, her "virginal tongue told" (stanza seventeen). The tears of sympathy she evokes are "a madrigal start"; this song or madrigal is the poem he is presently writing. "The Wreck of the Deutschland" is thus a poem about its own composition, a poem that explores and expounds its own coming into being. Among its principal themes is the meaning of poetic creation, presented in the relationship of the poet to the tall nun and in the nun's relationship to Christ; at the same time it calls into question the representation of this theme as a figurative presentation of what *must be* in theological terms and indeed *was* for Hopkins personally—"what refers to myself in the poem is all strictly and literally true and did all occur"—a literal event. The poem is thus about the successful realization of poetry and also about its impossibility.

The theme of writing is presented in many of the stanzas of "The Wreck of the Deutschland," and in much of Hopkins's greatest poetry, but in several stanzas the tropes Hopkins employs to present the narrative of the shipwreck reveal very clearly the problematic status of writing in the poem. One such stanza is the twenty-second:

> Five! the finding and sake
> And cipher of suffering Christ.
> Mark, the mark is of man's make
> And the word of it Sacrificed.
> But he scores it in scarlet himself on his own bespoken,
> Before-time-taken, dearest prizèd and priced—
> Stigma, signal, cinquefoil token
> For lettering of the lamb's fleece, ruddying of the rose-flake.

This stanza presents directly what other stanzas of the same poem and other poems that Hopkins was later to write present in less striking and immediately obvious ways: the central theme of Hopkins's works, the meaning, significance, and ontological status of language and of sign systems. "Cipher," "mark," "word," "stigma," "signal," "cinquefoil token," "lettering"—all these words indicate that representation, writing, and a general semiotic project are at issue in this stanza. They are balanced and opposed by another set of words— "suffering Christ," "Sacrificed," "lamb's fleece," and "rose-flake"—associated with religious tradition. The problem of religious tradition and belief is thus confronted by the theory of semiotics. In this confrontation the possibilities of writing poetry and of sustaining faith are tested. Both domains constrain each other, such that neither a general semiotic independent of faith nor a faith unconditioned by previously articulated sign systems (ordinary language, iconography) can be envisioned as a possibility by the poet.

The word "stigma" indicates this opposition quite well. It derives from the Greek στίγμα, meaning a "mark made by a pointed instrument," and refers in English specifically to the "marks resembling the wounds on the crucified body of Christ, said to have been supernaturally impressed on the bodies of certain saints and other devout persons" (OED). As the poem suggests, the word is a "signal," a sign, or, to recall the earlier word, "cipher" for "suffering Christ." But all signs must be "de-ciphered," must be made to yield up their signification, for their signification is determined relationally. Unless, of course, a sign is iconic, in Peirce's sense of the term, but this poem categorically rejects any such doctrine of the sign. The word "stigma" cannot be iconic, not only because iconic signs do not reside in language in Peirce's semiotics, but also because the word "stigma" points toward two rather different, even opposed, meanings. It refers, in ecclesiastical usage, to the marks left on Christ's body; hence, it is a sign of special divine favor (as in the case of St. Francis). But it also refers to "a mark made upon the skin by burning with a hot iron . . . , as a token of infamy or subjection; a brand"; hence, more generally, to any "mark of disgrace or infamy; a sign of severe censure or condemnation" (OED). Such a meaning is precisely the one that the Romans attached to the marks left on Christ's body, since for them he was a criminal, and crucifixion was the appropriate punishment for his offenses. Admittedly, the Christian tradition has radically altered the signification of this sign, but the suppressed meaning reemerges startlingly in Hopkins's poem.

The guilt in the poem is not Christ's, except in the sense that he has suffered to expiate the sins of mankind and thus assumed that guilt. The guilt is man's: "the mark is of man's make." This in a double sense, since the stigma in "The Wreck of the Deutschland" is represented by the five Franciscan nuns who were exiled from Germany by the Falck Laws and perished in the shipwreck. Like Christ, whose "cinquefoil token" they become, they are martyrs to religious oppression, innocent victims of human tyranny, but also of human sinfulness, which, in the Christian tradition, is the legacy of the Fall. The poem thus seems to concern the ancient question of theodicy, the problem of the existence of evil in the world despite the reign of Providence, here figured in the suffering and deaths of Christ and the five nuns. Like Milton, Hopkins lays the fault for

evil at the feet of man: "the mark is of man's make." But there is a difficulty here, one introduced by the next line: "And the word of it Sacrificed." The syntax makes the intention of this line unclear. Does the line
mean: "And the word that represents the mark is sacrificed?" In this
reading one would think that "word" would be capitalized, indicating the
English for St. John's *Logos*, that is, Christ himself who was sacrificed. A
more likely reading that avoids the troublesome difficulty of the absent
capital might substitute "As is" for "And" in the second line, suggesting
that both the mark (the stigma) and the word (Sacrificed) are man-made.
"Mark" and "word" are rendered equivalent, both words associated with
a kind of writing made visible in the figure of Christ's Crucifixion: "But
he scores it in scarlet himself on his own bespoken, / Before-time-taken,
dearest prizèd and priced." The word "he" should refer to man, since it
would be capitalized if it referred to God. And yet these two lines invite
such a heterodox reading, for the phrases "his own bespoken" and "dearest
prizèd and priced" surely remind the reader of the liturgical "His only
begotten Son." This reading is further suggested by the phrase "Before-
time-taken," which refers to the Scotist doctrine of the Incarnation.[2]
According to Scotus, Christ's Incarnation and Sacrifice was from eternity,
but the Fall of Man necessitated that the Sacrifice be bloody—a doctrine
that squares with the general point made in this poem that the suffering
of Christ, the marking of the stigma, is "of man's make." But here precisely
lies the difficulty: How can man have been responsible for the suffering
of Christ, and how can Christ have been man's "dearest prizèd and
priced" if he was indeed "Before-time-taken"? The theological complexities
are reflected in the syntactic and semantic ambiguities of these lines.

The subject of the stanza can be seen as the being of Christ in the
world and the relation of mankind to that being. Christ is both what man
is in the world and also something more, something other, an ontological
condition indicated by Hopkins's special sense of the word "sake" in the
opening line. Recall Hopkins's glossing of this word in a letter to Bridges
on the Purcell sonnet:

[2]Hopkins's reflections on the Scotist doctrine of the Incarnation occur in his retreat
notes for November 1881 (see S, 196-202). The crucial passage from Scotus's *Oxoniense* is
quoted by Father Devlin in his notes on these texts: "Sed ista imaginatio falsa est. . . . Et ideo
idem est Deum praedestinare et praedestinasse et praedestinaturum esse, et ita contingens
unum sicut aliud, quia nihil est nisi nunc aeternitatis mensurans illum actum, quod est nec
praesens nec praeteritum nec futurum, sed coexistens omnibus istis" (S, 306; ellipsis in the
text). Cf. Stephen Dedalus's more homely version: "What went forth to the ends of the
world to traverse not itself. God, the sun, Shakespeare, a commercial traveller, having itself
traversed in reality itself, becomes that self. . . . Self which it itself was ineluctably pre-
conditioned to become" (James Joyce, *Ulysses* [New York: Random House, 1934], p. 494).

It is the *sake* of "for the sake of," *forsake, namesake, keepsake.* I mean by it the being a thing has outside itself, as a voice by its echo, a face by its reflection, a body by its shadow, a man by his name, fame, or memory, *and also* that in the thing by virtue of which especially it has this being abroad, and that is something distinctive, marked, specifically or individually speaking, as for a voice and echo clearness; for a reflected image light, brightness; for a shadow-casting body bulk; for a man genius, great achievements, amiability, and so on. In this case it is, as the sonnet says, distinctive quality in genius. [L. I, 83]

The word "sake," like so many others in this stanza, has a double significance. It is the outward manifestation of an existent in the world, and it is also that inner quality which projects being into the world. Strange to think of Christ as a genius, but it is one characteristic, among others, that Hopkins associates with Him insofar as He has being in the world. The particular mark or sign of His being here is the stigma He bore at the Crucifixion which continues to be manifested in the world in St. Francis and the five nuns. The "name, fame, or memory" of Christ, the "sake" of His suffering, is the persistence of the sign, the stigma, in the saints and martyrs who bear His special mark. Christ is both in and out of the world, beyond it and yet vitally participating in it through the agency of those who bear the stigma of His suffering.

But what have these theological questions to do with the general semiotic project which I have said is the true theme of this stanza of "The Wreck of the Deutschland"? Just as Christ is both in and out of the world, of the world and beyond it, so language, or indeed any system of signs, including that system familiar to Hopkins in the iconographic traditions of Christianity, is similarly in the world, possessed of a kind of physical existence or presence (in speech), and out of the world, having an independent existence of its own beyond the particular articulations of any man or group of men (writing). Just as Christ is man-God, so language is speech-writing; just as Christ is perpetually re-presented in His martyrs and in the reappearance of the "stigma" in saints like Francis, so language perpetually reappears in the world in the persistence of writing. In this stanza, Hopkins describes the suffering and stigma of Christ as a kind of writing, an inscription "scored in scarlet." Like all inscriptions, this one requires interpretation, a deciphering, to be understood. Moreover, it is impossible to interpret this piece of writing without reference to the theological doctrines also presented in the stanza. This is not to say that interpretation simply takes as its reference point given meanings of certain signs from a body of fixed and coherent dogma. On the contrary, the poem reveals again and again the unstable condition of all signs, not only their polyvalence (which St. Augustine, and before him Plato, understood),[3] but their complete indeterminacy in the sense that no sign can remain forever unalterable as a fixed point of reference in relation to other signs.

All signs are determined by their relational value to other signs, and this value is in a state of perpetual flux. In the twenty-second stanza of "The Wreck of the Deutschland," the five Franciscan nuns, St. Francis, Christ, and the poet who records their deeds compose a field of inter-related signs that produce meaning in the spaces between them by an interaction that is ongoing and perpetual. To understand the significance of the death of the five nuns, it is not sufficient simply to work backwards through a linear chain of associations from the nuns to St. Francis to Christ and the Incarnation. The poem does not propose an historical succession with Christ at the zero point and the nuns at the end as the most recent incarnation of the pattern of Christ's suffering. It shows, rather, how the meaning of Christ's sacrifice is realized only in its various incarnations throughout history. As the phrase "Before-time-taken" with its suggestion of the Scotist doctrine of the Incarnation indicates, the Crucifixion itself fulfills the potential consequences of an anterior event. Each successive sacrifice modifies the meaning of all the previous ones at the same time that all earlier incarnations of the "suffering Christ" combine to illuminate the meaning of the last. Though the Crucifixion of Christ is historically prior to the death of the five Franciscan nuns, it can be said that the Crucifixion is only gradually completed in the succession of sacrifices which imitate and fulfill it. The full meaning of the Crucifixion is perpetually deferred as each new sacrifice resembles and imitates at the same time that it differs from all others that have preceded it.

The contention of Father Peters and others that Hopkins was a confirmed Scotist and that Hopkins's "inscape" is the equivalent of

---

[3]On the polyvalence of scripture and the doctrine of signs, see St. Augustine, *On Christian Doctrine*, trans. D. W. Robertson, Jr. (Indianapolis: Bobbs, Merrill, 1958), pp. 37-114. St. Augustine also comments on signs and on the difference between signs and truth in *De magistro*, English translation by George G. Leckie, *Concerning the Teacher and On the Immortality of the Soul* (New York: D. Appleton-Century, 1938), pp. 35-36. Though it can be argued that a theory of signs is the central question in all of Plato's thought, since the relation between sign and referent is precisely the difficulty presented in the theory of forms, the most explicit treatment of the linguistic sign occurs in the *Cratylus*, where the question of the origin of the meaning of signs is left unresolved.

Scotus's *haeccitas* can thus be seen to be in error.[4] If one understands Scotus, as Father Peters does, to propose a theory of the univocity of being, then nothing could be further from the beliefs presented in "The Wreck of the Deutschland." *Haeccitas* is not the equivalent of selving in Hopkins, for the being of each self is not merely subsumed in "the great monochrome abstraction of being" as it is in Scotus.[5] For Hopkins, being can in fact be said not to exist at all except in the differentiated beings who exist at any given moment in time. Moreover, the constitutive factor of time itself nullifies any univocal concept of being, for being is altered as history occurs by the emergence of new beings (individual selves—St. Francis, the nuns, the poet) and the disappearance of previous beings. Being, and similarly meaning in the poem, is the play of repetition and difference, the temporal recognition that different beings resemble each other and that resemblance can only be produced by difference.

The general semiotic project disclosed in the twenty-second stanza of "The Wreck of the Deutschland" is identical with the central theological question that haunts the entire poem: the difficulty of understanding the meaning of sacrifice, in the immediate instance the death of the five Franciscan nuns, but more generally the necessity for suffering in the world. By meditating in language upon the death of the five nuns, Hopkins attempts to unlock the "cipher of suffering Christ." But this cipher proves impossible to solve completely, for it points in two directions at once, neither of which can be left out of the account. "The mark is of man's make," but at the same time "he scores it is scarlet himself on his own bespoken / Before-time-taken, dearest prizèd and priced." Both man and God are responsible for the suffering of Christ and of the martyrs who follow Him. This double origin of Christ's suffering is never finally contradicted in the poem, which does not offer a definitive interpretation of Christ's suffering but links the death of the five nuns to the death of Christ and thus brings this last martyrdom into play as an element in the interpretation of the mystery of the Redemption. The death of the nuns does not bring to a close the process of understanding Christ's suffering; it offers yet another sign to be conjoined with earlier ones—Christ's death and suffering, St. Francis's suffering the stigmata, the deaths of

[4]See W.A.M. Peters, S.J., *Gerard Manley Hopkins* (London: Oxford University Press, 1948), pp. 22-23. See Father Devlin's refutation of Father Peters's contention in S, 293, 338-51.

[5]The phrase is quoted from the English translation of Michel Foucault's essay on Gilles Deleuze, "Theatrum Philosophicum," in Michel Foucault, *Language, Counter-Memory, Practice*, ed. Donald F. Bouchard, trans. Donald F. Bouchard and Sherry Simon (Ithaca: Cornell University Press, 1977), p. 187.

other martyrs—in a signifying structure that can never be completely resolved into a univocal and fixed meaning. Hopkins's poem can never finally resolve the "cipher of suffering Christ" because the signifying structure of which Christ is a part is never completed, the field of interpretation never closed off.[6]

Hopkins himself acknowledges the open signifying structure of his poetry in a letter to Bridges of November 6, 1887:

> My meaning surely *ought* to appear of itself; but in a language like English, an in an age of it like the present, written words are really matter open and indifferent to the receiving of different and alternative verse-forms, some of which the reader cannot possibly be sure are meant unless they are marked for him. . . . One thing I am now resolved on, it is to prefix short prose *arguments* to some of my pieces. . . . Epic and drama and ballad and many, most, things should be at once intelligible; but everything need not and cannot be. Plainly if it is possible to express a sub[t]le and recondite thought on a subtle and recondite subject in a subtle and recondite way and with a great felicity and perfection, in the end, something must be sacrificed, with so trying a task, in the process, and this may be the being at once, nay perhaps even the being without explanation at all, intelligible. Neither, in the same light, does it seem to me a real objection . . . that the argument should be even longer than the piece; for the merit of the work may lie for one thing in its terseness. It is like a mate which may be given, one way only, in three moves; otherwise, various ways, in many. [L. I, 265-66][7]

[6] Again a similar notion in Joyce presents itself. In the "Ithaca" section of *Ulysses*, Bloom reflects upon the impression of Boylan's form left on the clean bed sheets, and Joyce's scholastic interlocutor wryly notes the incongruity between the lover's self-image of his originality and the actuality of his position in a long series of amorous encounters extending far back in the past and on into the future: "Each one who enters imagines himself to be the first to enter whereas he is always the last term of a preceding series even if the first term of a succeeding one, each imagining himself to be first, last, only and alone, whereas he is neither first nor last nor only nor alone in a series originating in and repeated to infinity" (Joyce, *Ulysses*, p. 716). Though the ostensible subject here is Bloom's relation to Molly's carnal infidelities, insofar as Molly represents the Church and Bloom the mystical bridegroom (Christ), the representation of Christian history is exactly that envisioned by Hopkins in "The Wreck of the Deutschland."

[7] The generally unfavorable reception of Hopkins's poems when they first appeared in 1918 largely justifies the poet's apprehension over the difficulty that his language would cause readers. The early reviews are ably summarized in W. H. Gardner, *Gerard Manley Hopkins (1884-1889)*, 2 vols. (New Haven: Yale University Press, 1949), from which the following quotation, characteristic of the initial response to Hopkins's poetic style, is taken: "His adjectives not only at first reading but also at the tenth or twentieth, distract the mind

Hopkins is plainly aware of the syntactic and semantic difficulties of his poetry, difficulties that arise in part, he believes, from the imprecision and openness of language itself. He proposes to resolve this ambiguity in his own language by the addition of syntactic marks "as is done already partly in punctuation by everybody, partly in capitals by the Germans, more fully in accentuation by the Hebrews" (L. I, 265), and by affixing paraphrases to his poetry. But what would be the semantic status of such markings and prose glosses? Would the prose arguments constitute a primary signifying structure, a key to the codes of the poetry? That Hopkins never actually adopted these expedients for interpreting his poems suggests the futility of such an enterprise. The interpretive activity called forth by poetry cannot be arbitrarily halted by the infusion of some other form of writing into the interpretive field. A prose argument would, like any other piece of writing, demand interpretation itself; moreover, its exact relation to the poem to which it has been prefixed would also have to be examined, analyzed, resolved, an activity as problematic and potentially as complicated as the interpretation of the poem. In short, rather than simplifying and foreclosing interpretation, the insertion of further pieces of writing into the interpretive field complicates and extends the interpreter's activity.[8] Just as the sacrifice of the five Franciscan nuns does not complete once and for all the meaning of Christ's suffering, so appending an explanation to a poem does not foreclose the intepretive activity of the reader. The meaning of the poetic text is as unstable and various as the conclusion to a game of chess to which Hopkins analogizes his poetry at the end of this passage. In both, the real significance of the

---

altogether from their meaning by their strangeness. *Silk-sack clouds, azurous hung hills, majestic as a stallion stalwart, very-violet-sweet, mild night's blear-all black* and the like are traps for the attention, not aids to visualization" (Gardner, *Gerard Manley Hopkins*, 1: 213). Todd Bender characterizes the critical response, which he claims is dominated by the views expressed by Bridges in his preface to the first edition of the poems, as "not of resentment or hostility, but of bewilderment" (Todd K. Bender, *Gerard Manley Hopkins* [Baltimore: Johns Hopkins University Press, 1966], p. 9).

[8] This aspect of interpretation, the relationship of gloss to text, is itself glossed in Lawrence Lipking's essay, "The Marginal Gloss," *Critical Inquiry* 3 (Summer 1977): 609-55. Lipking's nostalgia for a simpler, more substantial, less "marginal" interpretive (interpreted?) world survives his attempt to bring Poe's "non-sense marginalia" into play in the text and the margins (the two are finally indistinguishable, as they are in Jacques Derrida's *Glas*, the model for Lipking's essay) of his criticism. Though Lipking is shrewd enough not to succumb to the temptation of proposing some specific ground or "degree zero" for interpretation, he nonetheless intimates that such an origin for the interpreter's glossing ought to be recoverable from a less complicated critical milieu in the past than our own. If Hopkins can serve as an example, the likelihood of such a past ever having existed is dubious.

game is produced by the sequence of moves (which changes from one playing to the next) rather than in the conclusion reached.[9]

The difficulty of interpretation, the question of how meaning can be produced, is the beginning, in the sense of the term developed by Edward Said, that gives rise to "The Wreck of the Deutschland." This beginning is dramatized in stanzas twenty-four and twenty-five, where the poet once again considers his relationship to the tall nun and tries to understand the significance of her cry at the height of the storm:

> Away in the loveable west
> On a pastoral forehead of Wales,
> I was under a roof here, I was at rest,
> And they the prey of the gales;
> She to the black-about air, to the breaker, the thickly
> Falling flakes, to the throng that catches and quails

---

[9]Hillis Miller has recently observed this problem of the openendedness of intepretation in "The Wreck of the Deutschland," arguing that it is represented in the poem by the implicit tension between nature on the one hand and language on the other: "There are indeed two texts in Hopkins, the overthought and the underthought. One text, the over-thought, is a version . . . of western metaphysics in its Catholic Christian form. In this text the Word governs all words, as it governs natural objects and selves. . . . On the other hand the underthought, if it is followed out, is a thought about language itself. It recognizes that there is no word for the Word, that all words are metaphors—that is, all are differentiated, differed, and deferred. Each leads to something of which it is the displacement in a movement without origin or end. Insofar as the play of language emerges as the basic model for the other two realms (nature and the effects of grace within the soul), it subverts both nature and supernature. The individual natural object and the individual self, by the fact of their individuality, are incapable of ever being more than a metaphor of Christ—that is, split off from Christ. They are incapable by whatever extravagant series of sideways transformations from ever becoming more than another metaphor" (Miller, "The Linguistic Moment in 'The Wreck of the Deutschland,'" in *The New Criticism and After*, ed. Thomas Daniel Young [Charlottesville: University Press of Virginia, 1976], p. 58). I would add to this admirable analysis only the observation that the figurative presentation of self and nature, of grace and the tall nun's experience of Christ, and of Hopkins's relationship to these objects and events is the poem itself. Thus, the underthought of "The Wreck of the Deutschland" is not simply "a thought about language itself" but about the specific realization in language of a psycho-linguistic event, the writing of the poem. This is not to say that there is some originating psychical principle that lies behind or is prior to the language of the poem, but that the poem is the scene of struggle between the poet and the tropes of language. "The Wreck of the Deutschland" is "about" Hopkins's will to master language and his realization of the degree to which he is finally and necessarily mastered by it.

>Was calling 'O Christ, Christ, come quickly':
>The cross to her she calls Christ to her, christens her wild-worst
>   Best.

>   The majesty! what did she mean?
>   Breathe, arch and original Breath.
>   Is it love in her of the being as her lover had been?
>   Breathe, body of lovely Death.
>   They were else-minded then, altogether, the men
>   Woke thee with a *We are perishing* in the weather of Gen-
>   nesareth.
>   Or is it that she cried for the crown then,
>   The keener to come at the comfort for feeling the combating
>   keen?

The contrast between the poet's protected, secure position ("I was under a roof here, I was at rest") and the peril in which the nuns stood is obvious enough. But "rest" here is particularly significant, suggesting the conventional Catholic opposition between the active and the contemplative life. The poet "at rest" resembles the figure in "The Windhover" who confesses his "heart in hiding." The suffering of the five nuns, and above all the call of the tall nun, will summon the poet into activity, will call him forth to the active life of the poet in search of meaning and style. What troubles the poet and provides the occasion for the entire poem is the difficulty of understanding the meaning of the tall nun's cry: "O Christ, Christ, come quickly." How, Hopkins wonders admiringly, could she transform her suffering into joy, christen "her wild-worst Best"? Her cry elicits the poet's admiration, but at virtually the same instant the cry becomes mysterious: "what did she mean?" To answer this question would unlock the mystery of faith, how the nun could apparently affirm the power of Christ's Redemption in the face of the most terrible adversity. Unlike the "else-minded" men who cried out in the storm "Lord save us! we are perishing!" and whom Christ rebuked, saying "Why are you fearful, O you of little faith?" (Matthew 8: 25-26)—unlike them, the tall nun "christens her wild-worst Best." Hopkins proposes a series of possible explanations, a number of interpretations of the nun's words: "Is it love in her of the being as her lover had been"; "or is it that she cried for the crown then, / The keener to come at the comfort for feeling the combating keen?" The representation of man's relationship to God in sexual imagery is a commonplace in Hopkins's poetry (see my discussion of the late poems in chapter 5), and as Gardner's note to this line indicates, the

relationship of Christ to the nun as lover is perfectly orthodox (P, 261).[10]
But in stanzas thirty and thirty-one, the figurative sexual relationship
between nun and Christ will be complicated by the poet's conflation of
the nun with the Blessed Virgin, thus making the nun both lover and
mother of Christ. And even though such imagery has the traditions of
Christian spirituality behind it, there is nonetheless something faintly
disquieting about the violence associated with such sexuality, just as
there is more than a trace of masochism in the concluding lines of stanza
twenty-five. Like Hopkins, who questions the mysterious meaning of the
nun's cry, the reader is led to wonder about the violence invoked in the
poet's figurative representation of the nun's supreme act of faith.

The theme of the violence of man's subjection to God's will has
recurred numerous times in the poem since the first stanza, where the
poet invokes the mastery of God in images of creation and destruction:
"Thou has bound bones and veins in me, fastened me flesh, / And after it
almost unmade, what with dread, / Thy doing: and dost thou touch me
afresh?" The emergence of faith presented metaphorically as parturition
first occurs in stanzas seven and eight:

> It dates from day
> Of his going in Galilee;
> Warm-laid grave of a womb-life grey;
> Manger, maiden's knee;
> The dense and the driven Passion, and frightful sweat:
> Thence the discharge of it, there its swelling to be,
> Though felt before, though in high flood yet—
> What none would have known of it, only the heart, being hard
>   at bay,
>
> Is out with it! Oh,
> We lash with the best or worst
> Word last!

Just as Christ is brought forth in the agony of childbirth, and just as he
suffered and died on the cross, so the faithful Christian affirms his faith in

---

[10]Cf. M. H. Abrams on Wordsworth's "spousal verse" of the apocalyptic marriage
between heaven and earth: "So thoroughly was the figure of Christ the Bridegroom
interinvolved with the concept of Christ the Redeemer, that commentators early inaugurated
the tradition that Christ's words on the cross ('*consummatum est*' in the Vulgate, John 19:
30) signified that Christ mounted the cross as a bed on which to consummate the marriage
with humanity inaugurated at the Incarnation, in the supreme act of sacrifice which both
certified and prefigured His apocalyptic marriage at the end of time" (M. H. Abrams,
Natural Supernaturalism [New York: W. W. Norton, 1971], p. 45).

an act of stressful, painful, violent bringing forth of—and this is crucial
—the Word. What Mary brought into the world was Christ, the Word,
Logos; similarly, the cry of the tall nun is a "wording" of her faith, an act
resembling the conception and parturition of Christ. Christ as *Logos*, the
nun as imitator of the Blessed Virgin, the importance of wording *the*
Word, of speaking Christ's name and reaffirming one's faith in his Redemption—these figural images of the nun's significance are carefully
orchestrated in stanzas twenty-nine and thirty:

> Ah! there was a heart right!
> There was single eye!
> Read the unshapeable shock night
> And knew the who and the why;
> Wording it how but by him that present and past,
> Heaven and earth are word of, worded by?—
> The Simon Peter of a soul! to the blast
> Tarpeïan-fast, but a blown beacon of light.
>
> Jesu, heart's light,
> Jesu, maid's son,
> What was the feast followed the night
> Thou hadst glory of this nun?—
> Feast of the one woman without stain.
> For so conceivèd, so to conceive thee is done;
> But here was heart-throe, birth of a brain
> Word, that heard and kept thee and uttered thee outright.

The answer to the question posed in stanza twenty-five, "what did she
mean?," is given in the figures of suffering, violence, conception, and
parturition in stanzas thirty and thirty-one. The meaning of the nun's cry
is the same as the meaning of Mary's giving birth to Christ and as the
meaning of the Crucifixion itself.

But what exactly is the suffering experienced by Christ? And what
does it signify to say that the call of the nun resembles the parturition of
the Word through the Blessed Virgin? To refer the signification of the
nun's cry back to these apparently primary significations is not at all to
solve the mystery of her utterance. For the Immaculate Conception, the
Annunciation, the Incarnation, the Crucifixion, and the Redemption are
all mysteries of faith which can only be understood (if indeed they can be
properly said to be "understood" at all) in relation to each other. All the
figures for the nun's cry are as much signifiers whose signification remains

in question as the nun's cry itself. To interpret the nun's words, Hopkins must comprehend all the mysteries of Christianity—and that is what the entire poem strives desperately to do! Hopkins is thrown back once again upon his original question, "what did she mean?," but with an enlarged conception of the scope of the question itself. Moreover, the elaboration of a series of answers to this primary question has raised the fundamental hermeneutical problem of the poem: What does it mean to mean? How, in short, does one achieve knowledge; what are the processes by which one comes to decipher the signification of any utterance? The poet is faced with the general semiotic project proposed in, among other places, the twenty-second stanza of the poem, a project which, as I have suggested, is inseparable from the theological problems presented by the poem as a whole and by the language burdened with the weight of religious tradition that Hopkins falls into whenever he represents an event or an idea or an object. Another way of putting this is to say that the true subject of "The Wreck of the Deutschland" is "wording" in all the complex and polyvalent significations that swirl around this signifier in the poem.

In the poem's opening stanza, Hopkins exclaims:

> Thou mastering me
> God! giver of breath and bread;
> World's strand, sway of the sea;
> Lord of living and dead.

The metaphor of God as the "giver of breath" and "Lord of living and dead" is repeated in stanza twenty-five: "Breathe, arch and original Breath. / . . . Breathe, body of lovely Death." The lines undoubtedly refer, as Gardner's note indicates (P, 261), to Genesis 2: 7: "Then the Lord God formed man out of the dust of the ground and breathed into his nostrils the breath of life, and man became a living being." God's "inspiration" gives man life. I have chosen this word advisedly, with a proper sense of the pun involved, since in "The Wreck of the Deutschland" the creation of man is a metonymy for poetic creation. God masters the poet, disciplines him, shapes and forms his soul, gives birth to him as a poet in short. The figure of God in the poem is at once the divinity of Christianity and the demon of poetic form with whom Hopkins will later find himself locked in a life and death struggle (see chapter 5, the discussion of the poet's wrestling with his god in "Carrion Comfort"). The poet's fearful experience of divine presence in stanzas one and two figuratively presents the psychic battle of the poet with form:

Thou has bound bones and veins in me, fastened me flesh,
And after it almost unmade, what with dread,
Thy doing: and dost thou touch me afresh?
Over again I feel thy finger and find thee.

I did say yes
O at lightning and lashed rod;
Thou heardst me truer than tongue confess
Thy terror, O Christ, O God;
Thou knowest the walls, altar and hour and night:
The swoon of a heart that the sweep and the hurl of thee trod
Hard down with a horror of height:
And the midriff astrain with leaning of, laced with fire of stress.

The making and unmaking (we might instructively compare this image to Yeats's endless stitching and unstitching) is the poet's perpetual confrontation with language, with an original and energetic style which he must strain to attain, for it is "laced with fire of stress." "Stress" is the crucial concept in Hopkins's discovery of sprung rhythm, as Father Ong has shown. The strain of words against their normal intonation, and against their ordinary semantic and syntactic usage, necessarily follows from the use of sprung rhythm. Hopkins's stylistic achievement is a reorientation of the patterns of energy in the English poetic line, that causes meaning to burst forth, explode, from the concentration of rhythmic and lexical power in a single syllable, an effect Hopkins believed could not be produced by ordinary running rhythm. The explosive potential of the single word realized in Hopkins's new rhythm is represented by the image of the bursting sloe in stanza eight:

Oh,
We lash with the best or worst
Word last! How a lush-kept plush-capped sloe
Will, mouthed to flesh-burst,
Gush!—flush the man, the being with it, sour or sweet,
Brim, in a flash, full!

The same effect is achieved in "The Windhover" in the gathering together of the rhythm and syntax of the poem into the single word "Buckle." The flashing, flaming, explosive properties of language are exploited and enhanced in Hopkins's poetry. His style, forged by the strenuous spiritual effort depicted in the first ten stanzas of this poem, is "charged with the grandeur of God. / It will flame out, like shining from shook foil; / It gathers to a greatness, like the ooze of oil / Crushed" (P, 66).

"The Wreck of the Deutschland" is best read, then, as a poem about poetic creation, about the extremities of the poet's battle to realize a personal style and to be equal to the demands of the powerfully mastering demon of poetic form. As many commentators have noted, the crucial moment in this struggle comes in stanza twenty-eight, with the appearance of Christ to the tall nun:

> But how shall I . . . make me room there:
> Reach me a . . . Fancy, come faster—
> Strike you the sight of it? look at it loom there,
> Thing that she . . . There then! the Master,
> *Ipse*, the only one, Christ, King, Head:
> He was to cure the extremity where he had cast her;
> Do, deal, lord it with living and dead;
> Let him ride, her pride, in his triumph, despatch and have done
> with his doom there.

The severe control of rhythm and syntax that characterizes the rest of the poem vanishes here, as the poet gropes toward the representation of the nun's vision of Christ. Hillis Miller's commentary on these lines is apt:

> The tragic limitation of poetic language lies in the fact that the Word itself cannot be said. . . . A word by the very fact that it is just that pattern of vowels and consonants which it is, cannot be the Word. The words of human language, for Hopkins, seem to have been born of some primal division, a fall from the arch and original breath into the articulate. This fall has always already occurred as soon as there is any human speech. Words have therefore a tendency to proliferate endlessly their permutations by changes of vowel and consonant as if they were in search for the magic word that would be the Word.[11]

Miller's insight into the poet's struggle with language is acute. The aposiopeses signify the difficulty of expressing in language the presence of Christ before the nun. The series of names for Christ ("the Master, / *Ipse*, the only one, Christ, King, Head") shows how the denominating

[11]Miller, "The Linguistic Moment in 'The Wreck of the Deutschland,'" p. 56. Elisabeth Schneider also recognizes the pivotal position of stanza twenty-eight in the poem, arguing that Hopkins's loss of syntactic control is the result of his attempt to represent a "miraculous event," viz. Christ's appearance before the tall nun (see Elisabeth Schneider, *The Dragon in the Gate*, pp. 29-32).

function of language can only produce a proliferating chain of figurative expressions for the thing named. No single expression is primary or original, giving rise to all the others; the words are merely metonymic substitutions for each other. But it is not only the general struggle of the poet with language that is metaphorically presented in this stanza, but a specific event in the poet's career. The "I" of the first line refers to Hopkins's emerging poetic self in "The Wreck of the Deutschland." The question of how the poet "shall . . . make me room there" is the central problem that the poem has raised in other ways from the beginning. How can the imagination envision the scene of the nun's miraculous calling down of Christ upon herself? How can the poem interpret rhetorically the nun's cry, "O Christ, Christ, come quickly"? How can the poem that re-presents and re-creates this experience come to be at all? To envision the scene of the nun's call is to interpret its meaning, which is to create imaginatively—figuratively, rhetorically, in tropes—the moment of the nun's vision of Christ. Thus, the poet's psychic-rhetorical struggle, the scene of the poem he is writing, is identical with the nun's miraculous vision. The language of the last three lines of this stanza reinforces the poet's imitation of the nun's martyrdom by recalling the figures of earlier stanzas in which the poet presented his personal confrontation with God, the lord of living and dead, Christ riding in triumph. Hopkins here "words" the nun's vision, just as she herself had "worded" Christ and been worded by Him. To "word" is to create and to be created in that paradoxical, double condition of mastery and mercy wherein the poet discovers himself as begetter and begotten of a personal style.

The fruit of this confrontation with language and style extends beyond the poem itself to engender the birth of the poet into his career. At the end of the thirty-first stanza, Hopkins asks: "Is the shipwrack then a harvest, does tempest carry the grain for thee?" These two metaphors will come to dominate Hopkins's later writings as figures for poetic failure and poetic achievement respectively. As Hopkins remarked in a letter to his friend Baillie written during the last years of his life: "There they lie and my old notebooks and beginnings of things, ever so many, which it seems to me might well have been done, ruins and wrecks; but on this theme I will not enlarge by pen and ink" (L. III, 255). Of course Hopkins did greatly "enlarge by pen and ink" on this painful theme in his last poems; at the end of his life he could write about nothing else. Even in "The Wreck of the Deutschland," he was acutely conscious of the stringent demands placed upon the writer by his desire to create and of the spiritual constraint produced by the achievement of great poetry. The great strength of this poem that distinguishes and separates it from all Hopkins's subsequent poems is its striving toward the Sublime and its discovery of the enormous cost of such striving. "The Wreck of the Deutschland" never wavers in its portrayal of the suffering, pain, and loss necessary to bring the poet to his desired goal. In the poem, this realization is symbolized most graphically in the suffering and death of the tall nun. Her martyrdom is not merely the occasion for the poem but also the allegorical sign for the poet's attainment of the Sublime.

In what sense does "The Wreck of the Deutschland" aim at and attain sublimity? Potentially, this question would demand a long and detailed inquiry into the category of the Sublime, a detour that would chart the history of aesthetic theory from the pseudo-Longinus to Burke and Kant through Schiller and Coleridge and finally to Ruskin, and would trace the development of English poetry from Milton to Blake and Wordsworth through Shelley and thence to Hopkins. I have no intention of undertaking such a monumental inquiry here, but I can indicate the general character of the Sublime in "The Wreck of the Deutschland" and the terrible burden that the attainment of this mode placed upon Hopkins's ensuing career. Thomas Weiskel has described very well the significance of the Romantic Sublime, its emergence at an historical moment when the possibility of transcendence seemed increasingly tenuous:

> The Romantic sublime was an attempt to revise the meaning of transcendence precisely when the traditional apparatus of sublimation—spiritual, ontological, and (one gathers) psychological and even perceptional—was failing to be exercised or understood. It was the most spectacular response of the literary mind to the dualisms which cut across post-Renaissance thinking and made so much authoritative doctrine suddenly in need of interpretation. It was not least a hermeneutic, a remarkably successful way to read, offering formulas which preserved the authority of the past within the ramified strictures of dualism. It provided a language for urgent and apparently novel experiences of anxiety and excitement which were in need of legitimation. In largest perspective, it was a major analogy, a massive transposition of transcendence into a naturalistic key; in short a stunning metaphor.[12]

This "massive transposition of transcendence into a naturalistic key," which attained its zenith, according to Weiskel, in Wordsworth's "ego-

[12]Weiskel, *The Romantic Sublime* (Baltimore: Johns Hopkins University Press, 1976), p. 4.

tistical Sublime," was for Hopkins accomplished in the nun's martyrdom
and in the poet's submission to the mastering power of formal constraints.
The Sublime consists for Hopkins in the representation of the nun's
vision of Christ and in her affirmation of the Crucifixion and Redemption
in the language of the poem. This touching of the divine finds figurative
expression in the twenty-first stanza of "The Wreck of the Deutschland,"
where Hopkins represents the transformation of the hostile forces of
nature into figures of comfort through the agency of divine vision:

> Surf, snow, river and earth
> Gnashed: but thou are above, thou Orion of light;
> Thy unchancelling poising palms were weighing the worth,
> Thou martyr-master: in thy sight
> Storm flakes were scroll-leaved flowers, lily showers—sweet
> heaven was astrew in them.

Hopkins's representation of the death of the five nuns transfigures their
physical suffering and thus naturalizes, in the language of the poem, the
divine intervention which he recognizes as the transformative power in
their martyrdom. For Hopkins, transcendence becomes the property of
the poetic imagination, just as the tall nun transforms her suffering into
salvation by "wording" Christ, by affirming her faith in transcendence
when she cries out: "O Christ, Christ, come quickly."

But there is a danger latent in the naturalization of the divine, a
danger imperiling the imagination which Hopkins saw only too clearly.
As Ruskin recognized so well, the propensity of the imagination to revel
in sublimity was among its most frightening tendencies:

> For though it is the nature of the imagination to rouse itself with little
> help, yet it will never start but from the highest point it can reach; its
> ambition is insatiable; it always fixes on the largest thing it has in
> sight; and if, presently, anything still greater be offered to it, it flies to
> that, and instantly spurns what it before thought majestic. And this
> avarice of the imagination increases with the stimulus; and the more
> it obtains, the more it conceives it possible to obtain; and it may be
> pushed at last into a morbid hunger, in which it has nearly lost its
> own inherent power, but continually craves an increase of external
> excitement—and at last dies of pure repletion.[13]

[13]Ruskin, *The Works of John Ruskin*, ed. E. T. Cook and Alexander Wedderburn,
Library Ed., 39 vols. (London: G. Allen, 1903-1912), 5: 436. On the tendency of the mind
and the language of the poet to draw back from the excessive fullness of imagination
attained in the Sublime, see Neil Hertz, "The Notion of Blockage in the Literature of the
Sublime," in *Psychoanalysis and the Question of the Text*, ed. Geoffrey H. Hartman
(Baltimore: Johns Hopkins University Press, 1978), pp. 62-85.

Hopkins greatly feared "this avarice of the imagination," as his ambivalence toward poetry in the letter to Dixon about the genesis of "The Wreck of the Deutschland" shows. Poetry always remained for Hopkins perilously close to the song of Lucifer, a "dwelling on his own beauty, an instressing of his own inscape, and like a performance on the organ and instrument of his own being; it was a sounding . . . of his own trumpet and a hymn in his own praise" (S, 201). Hopkins never allowed his imagination the free rein that Ruskin believed would lead to its death "of pure repletion." Quite the contrary, as the poetry after "The Wreck of the Deutschland" shows, his response to the attainment of the Sublime was an immediate curtailment of his imaginative energy, a willful restriction of his poetic powers within the most demanding and disciplined of English verse forms, the sonnet. The insistent bad conscience which plagues the Romantic imagination and which Harold Bloom has labeled the anxiety of influence led Hopkins to a scrupulous revision of himself, to an even more severe *askesis* than he had practiced in "The Wreck of the Deutschland." The "ruins and wrecks" of his later career resulted from his too successful quest for the Sublime in his first and only poem in this mode. Hopkins emerged from this early dark night of the soul strong and invigorated with creative energy, the evidence for which is the explosion of poetic exuberance in the sonnets of 1877. But like Jacob, who limped forever after wrestling with the angel, Hopkins was permanently marked with the stylistic oddities imposed by the strain of creating himself as a poet. The extraordinary strength of this style and the necessity for limiting and controlling it is presented with greatest clarity in Hopkins's most celebrated and most celebratory poem, "The Windhover."

A Short Note in Lieu of an Interchapter

IT HAS BEEN THE CUSTOM TO REGARD the poems written during the two years following the composition of "The Wreck of the Deutschland," generally referred to as "the nature sonnets," as the most exuberant, the most joyful, the most affirmative Hopkins ever wrote. Most readers have emphasized the "juice" and "joy" of "Spring" and the "glory" of "dappled things" celebrated in "Pied Beauty." But what has gone largely unremarked is the gathering in of the stylistic extravagance of "The Wreck of the Deutschland," the limitation of Hopkins's formal experiments within the comparatively constricted boundaries of the sonnet. This is most evident in "Pied Beauty," in which the fourteen lines of the traditional sonnet are further curtailed while keeping, Hopkins thought, the mathematical relations between the parts which give the sonnet its peculiar structural power. Rather than celebrate the glorious oozings of "God's Grandeur," I would like to characterize these poems with an image from the title of one of their number—the caged skylark. Unlike Shelley's "blithe spirit," Hopkins's symbol of the poet suggests limitation, entrapment, a kind of stifling imprisonment of the spirit. Hopkins's repeated attempts to free himself from the constraints of his, in part, self-created cage produced only smaller and smaller cages to contain his stylistic energies, until in the end, the bird had not sufficient room to sing.

V   "MY WINTER WORLD":
HOPKINS'S LATE POEMS

It is tempting when talking about Hopkins's later career as a poet to let poems like the "terrible sonnets" and "Carrion Comfort" speak for themselves. Even a casual reading of these poems produces a sense of the poet's agonized spiritual suffering. And when read in the context of the letters and private notes written by Hopkins during the same period in his life, these poems seem undeniably to testify to the poet's personal mental crisis during his last years. One feels almost presumptuous to comment upon the poems at all, for their eloquent depiction of Hopkins's tortured soul requires no commentary. What could one say about Hopkins's state of mind that is not said with incomparably greater precision and grace by the poems themselves? But to proceed in this way is to assume that the meaning and purpose of these poems, and of poetry in general, is to portray the psyche of the poet. Poetry thus performs, in the terminology of M. H. Abrams, an expressive function. It would of course be foolish to deny such a meaning to Hopkins's late poems, for they are indeed documents in the spiritual life of the man Gerard Manley Hopkins. On the other hand, to say so is not to exhaust their significance. All men suffer psychic grief, but only a few write poems in which their grief is portrayed. To say that Hopkins's late poems are about his personal mental crisis is only the first step toward understanding them. They are expressions of a special subjectivity, the nature of which is by no means simple.

The nature of the subject or the self is, as I have argued in chapter 3, a difficult point for Hopkins. These complexities of the self in Hopkins are thrown into relief by a recent exchange between Hillis Miller and Kenneth Burke. Responding the Burke's contention that the word "wreck" in "The Wreck of the Deutschland" refers to Hopkins's personal wreck and that this idea provides the key to understanding Hopkins's poetry, Miller argues that such an attempt "to relate the linguistic complexities, or tensions, back to their subjective counterparts" conceals a number of questionable assumptions about the nature of poems and also about subjectivity:

The danger in Burke's suggestion . . . is, as always, the possibility of a psychologizing reduction, the making of literature into no more than a reflection or representation of something psychic which precedes it and which could not exist without it. I should prefer to see Hopkins's personal wreck as his inextricable involvement, "in flesh and in blood," in a chain or net of signs, figures, concepts, and narrative patterns. The exchanges, permutations, contradictions, latent aporias, untyings and typings of these elements he had the courage and the genius to "live through" in his writing and in his experience. Subjectivity, I am arguing, with all its intensities, is more a result than an origin. To set it first, to make an explanatory principle of it, is, as Nietzsche says, a metalepsis, putting late before early, effect before cause.[1]

The same point must be made about Hopkins's late poems. They are undoubtedly chapters in the history of the poet's self, but this history is told in texts that render equivocal the very concept of the self they seek to explain. Just as, I have argued, the flight of the windhover does not merely refer to an event in nature, or to the system of signs in Christian iconography, but represents the activity of the poet in creating, "the achieve of, the mastery of," the poem, so the self represented in Hopkins's late poems is radically textual. If these poems mean anything at all, it is that the self can only be produced in the writing of the poem. There is no self behind or prior to the poem which is responsible for the poem's existence. The self *is* the poem as it struggles to emerge out of the chaos of sensations and images that threaten at every moment to overwhelm it and reduce it to meaningless babble. For the poet, there can be no selfhood without this struggle toward meaning that "fathers-forth" the poem.

One of Hopkins's most poignant realizations of a poetic self is the first of the truly dark poems that dominate his later career. "Spelt from Sibyl's Leaves" (P, 97-98) powerfully dramatizes the extremity of the poet's effort to achieve what D. H. Lawrence called "verbal consciousness," though it is an open question whether this effort has succeeded or failed. I strongly suspect that the poem is more an expression of the will to meaning than an achievement of significance. Ostensibly, the subject of the poem is apocalypse and the last judgment; it depicts the twilight of the world on the eve of its dissolution and perhaps, at the end, a vision of

[1]Miller, "The Linguistic Moment in 'The Wreck of the Deutschland,'" in *The New Criticism and After*, ed. Thomas Daniel Young (Charlottesville: University Press of Virginia, 1976), pp. 59-60.

the damned in hell. It is a melancholy and even frightening poem, the more so because its vision is prophetic, a prediction of the world's future "spelt from Sibyl's leaves." Moreover, the poem marks a departure in tone from the poems Hopkins had been writing previously.[2] The reader of Hopkins's poetry is led to wonder what had changed in Hopkins to make him compose such a bleak and forbidding image of the world where the gloriously dappled qualities of things, celebrated in earlier poems, have vanished: "For earth / her being has unbound; her dapple is at an end." Paul Mariani's reading of the poem as "an Ignatian meditation on the state of hell" suggests that the melancholy picture of the world is simply the proper image to be conjured up during this meditation. In focusing only on images of desolation, Hopkins is following the injunction of St. Ignatius: "In meditating on a desolate subject, the exercitant is not to summon up images of consolation. And Hopkins does not."[3] But this explanation begs the question, since it does not account for why such a meditation came to occupy Hopkins at this moment in his life but did not two years earlier. One answer would be that the poem is a reflection of Hopkins's profound unhappiness in his new post as fellow in classics at the Royal University in Dublin. Hopkins disliked Dublin and despised his duties from the first (see L. I, 189-90), and the poem can be seen to originate in part in the crisis in his mental life that ensued upon his appointment to the Dublin post. And yet, to recall the argument made by Hillis Miller against Kenneth Burke, this explanation of the poem's genesis may be a confusion of cause and effect, for it may be that the composition of this and subsequent poems engendered Hopkins's spiritual crisis, rather than the other way around. I do not wish to take Miller's side in this dispute, any more than I wish to take Burke's. The poem, as both representation of the psyche and as "linguistic moment," should be preserved in any reading of Hopkins's late poems, for the poems originate and play out their tragic contradictions in the dialectic between these two aspects of writing. To determine which is cause and which effect is not possible, since Hopkins's spiritual life and his poetry are finally inseparable.

[2]Gardner dates the poem early in 1885, contemporary with the writing of Caradoc's soliloquy from "St. Winifred's Well" (P, 284). Hopkins thus did not complete any poems between "The Blessed Virgin compared to the Air we Breathe," written in May 1883, and "Spelt from Sibyl's Leaves" in 1885. The nearly two years separating these poems mark one of the most significant moments in Hopkins's career, an important hiatus during which Hopkins's world of "Wild air, world-mothering air" (P, 93) is transformed into "Earnest, earthless, equal, attuneable, vaulty, voluminous, . . . stupendous / Evening."

[3]Mariani, *Commentary on the Complete Poems of Hopkins* (Ithaca: Cornell University Press, 1970), pp. 199, 209.

This may at first seem a perverse point to make about "Spelt from Sibyl's Leaves." The poem appears so obviously to concern matters other than the writing of poetry. The subject of the poem is apocalypse, a prophetic vision originating—but *that* is the question! Whence comes this vision of the world on the eve of apocalypse and last judgment? If the closing lines depict the suffering of the damned in hell, what is the source of the poet's knowledge? It can be argued, along lines laid out by Paul Mariani, that the imagery is conventional, taken over from the *Spiritual Exercises*, but this reading ignores what the poem proclaims in its title: that the poet's vision originates in the "leaves" of the Sibyl. But how does one gain knowledge from the Sibyl, how is the vision of the poem "spelt" from her "leaves"? As Gary Stonum has rightly put it, "the poem is as concerned with the activity of telling and spelling as it is with the knowledge thus achieved or the springs of that knowledge."[4] "Spelt" is an important and complicated word. In a dialectical form, it refers to the activity of threshing: "To husk or pound (grain); to bruise or split (*esp.* beans)" (OED). This image accords well with the portrayal of the last judgment, the division of souls into the blessed and the damned, the separation of fruit from chaff. It also recalls the opening stanza of an earlier poem, "Barnfloor and Winepress," in which the Redemption is represented in traditional Christian images of the harvest and threshing (see P, 16-17). Understood in this way, "spelt" also looks forward to the image in "Carrion Comfort" that exemplifies the poet's understanding of his affliction by powers outside himself. "Why" he asks, "am I so afflicted?": "That my chaff might fly; my grain lie, sheer and clear" (P, 100). "To spell" can also mean: "To discover or find out, to guess or suspect, by close study or observation"; and "To make out, understand, decipher, or comprehend, by study" (OED). "Spelling" thus indicates the interpretive effort that the poem accomplishes; the "leaves" from which the poem's vision is "spelt" must be the leaves of the *Sibylline Books* which were enshrined in the Capitol in ancient Rome. This meaning of "spelt" links the poem to the tradition of the sibyl's prophetic witnessing of the last judgment, expressed in the lines from the *Dies Irae* sung at Requiem Mass: "Dies irae, dies illa / Solvet saeclum in favilla: / Teste David cum Sibylla." But there is yet a third possible meaning for this word, one which suggests that the poem is a kind of incantation. "To spell" also means: "To charm, fascinate, bewitch, bind by (or as by) a spell; to act as a spell upon"; and "to protect (one) *from* to drive *away*, by means of a

---

[4]Gary Stonum, "The Hermeneutics of 'Spelt from Sibyl's Leaves,'" *Hopkins Quarterly* 3 (1976): 117.

spell or charm" (OED). Understood in this way "Spelt from Sibyl's Leaves"
is an incantatory postponement of the *dies irae* represented in its lines, a
means of staving off the inevitable moment of death and judgment, a
prayer if you will. In each of these meanings, "spelt" indicates an ongoing
activity in the poem, be it separating and dividing, interpreting and
deciphering, or chanting and charming. What the poem is about, then, is
once again its own coming into being, its threshing, deciphering, putting
a spell upon the poet. This poem, like so many of Hopkins's major lyrics
and like his great ode, is a poetic autobiography, an anatomy of the
poet's struggle with language.

That "Spelt from Sibyl's Leaves" was in some measure an experiment
in poetic virtuosity is clear from Hopkins's famous letter to Bridges in
which the poem is termed "the longest sonnet ever made" (L. I, 246). The
unusual "length" of the sonnet is produced by the eight full stresses
intoned in each line. This odd meter makes each line the equivalent in
time of two ordinary poetic lines, a fact Hopkins acknowledges by
marking the caesura between the fourth and fifth stresses. The metrical
scheme makes the poem very difficult to recite, though Hopkins claimed,
in the letter to Bridges cited above, that only in careful and attentive
recitation could the full effect of the poem be achieved. The tendency in
reading the poem is to separate each word into a unit of stress and
meaning. This is especially the case in the first two lines: "Earnest, earth-
less, equal, attuneable, | vaulty, voluminous, . . . stupendous / Evening
strains to be tíme's vást, | womb-of-all, home-of-all, hearse-of-all night."
In these lines, only the words "to" and "be" do not receive primary stress;
each word is a virtually self-contained moment exploding into meaning.
The grammatical connection between the seven adjectives of the first line
and "evening" in the second is almost entirely obscured by the stress
pattern of the poem. The first lines are broken up into virtually unrelated
units of sound and meaning. The language of the poem thus reproduces
in its own tendency toward disarticulation or dismemberment the theme
of nature's dissolution announced in the last four lines of the octet:

> For earth | her being has unbound: her
>   dapple is at an end, as-
> tray or aswarm, all throughther, in throngs; | self ín self
>   steepèd and páshed—qúite
> Disremembering, dísmémbering | áll now. Heart, you round
>   me right
> With: Óur évening is over us; óur night | whélms, whélms,
>   ánd will end us.

Just as nature is dissolving into its elements, so the poem is strained to the breaking point, its unity and coherence shattered by the rhythmic pressure of the eight-stress line. Every line is so packed with stress that it spills over into another line, as if the poetic line itself cannot contain all that the words wish to say. Even individual words, like "astray," cannot finally be held together, but break into two units separated by the division of one line from another. Nature, the poem, and even language itself are coming apart at the seams.

The sestet reinforces the "bleakness" and "blackness" suggested in the closing line of the octet and elaborates the spiritual consequences of this vision: the division of all creation into two groups, "black, white; ǀ right, wrong"; and the suffering of the damned in hell. The latter image is present in the final lines: "of a rack / Where, selfwrung, selfstrung, sheathe-and shelterless, ǀ thóughts agaínst thoughts ín groans grínd." As numerous commentators have noticed, this image corresponds to Hopkins's description of the agonized conscience of the damned in his "Meditation on Hell": "[They feel] the worm of conscience, which is the mind gnawing and feeding on its own most miserable self" (S, 243). Gardner remarks on the unusual stresses dictated by this meaning in the final line: "The stress on *against* emphasizes the painful friction and renders necessary the unusual stress on *in*" (P, 285). But the "painful friction" indicated here is not simply the representation of a state of the soul outside the poem. The entire poem exhibits the friction, the winding, the unbinding, the straining of the poet against his own language. The "rack" on which "thóughts agaínst thoughts ín groans grínd" is the poetic structure against which Hopkins contends and which finally impels the poem's dissolution into the harsh, guttural sounds of the final words. It is worth recalling here Hopkins's early etymological note on the root significance of the initial sound "gr": "*Grind, gride, gird, grit, groat, grate, greet* . . . etc. Original meaning to *strike, rub*, particularly *together*" (J, 5). The "painful friction" in these lines is to a large extent a linguistic friction, a "rubbing together" or "striking" of one word against another such that cohesiveness, fluidity, and formal regularity are shattered. The linguistic torture of "Spelt from Sibyl's Leaves" is thus the perfect prelude to the poems Hopkins was about to write. Its linguistic virtuosity, its rhythmic difficulty, its message of an impending "dark night of the soul"—all these frequently remarked aspects of the poem can be seen as the poet's titanic struggle with his vocation, his blighted quest to become once again the poet he was always striving to be. "The achieve of, the mastery of the thing" in "The Windhover" gives way in this and subsequent poems to the straining eunuch of "Thou art indeed just, Lord," who is unable to "breed one work that wakes" (P, 106-7).

There is an unmistakable irony in such a profession by the poet, for all the time he bemoans his creativity and his inability to bring forth poetry, he is doing so in poetry. Poems continue to be written, though increasingly their theme is the poet's lack of inspiration, his waning creative power. This very paradox is the subject of Hopkins's sonnet "To R. B.," which Hopkins wrote less than two months before his death. Perhaps no other poet of the last two centuries, with the possible exception of Keats in "This living hand," has written so movingly of the end of his poetic career on the eve of his actual death. Put simply, the poem is Hopkins's apology to Bridges for not having written more, and also for no longer producing verse in his characteristic style:

O then if in my lagging lines you miss

The roll, the rise, the carol, the creation,
My winter world, that scarcely breathes that bliss
Now, yields you, with some sighs, our explanation. [P, 108]

Hopkins's "lagging lines" lack the "roll, the rise, the carol" of his earlier poetry in which vigorous rhythmic structure marked his special style as a poet. It is true that his last poems, with only a few exceptions, do not possess the metrical originality or the strength of a personal style characteristic of his best poetry, and this is especially the case in "To R. B." As Hopkins himself admits, the "fire" has gone out of his poetry: "Sweet fire the sire of muse, my soul needs this; / I want the one rapture of an inspiration."

Fire and breath—these are the two qualities absent from Hopkins's last poems. Fire is the ubiquitous symbol of creativity and energy in Hopkins's writings. The "lightning and lashed rod" of "The Wreck of the Deutschland," the "grandeur of God" which "will flame out like shining from shook foil," the "Heraclitean fire" of the poem of that title, and the famous opening line "As kingfishers catch fire, dragonflies draw flame" —these and many other instances can be cited to illustrate Hopkins's imaging of creative energy and what he called "selving" in fire. As he remarks in his commentary on the *Spiritual Exercises*: "All things therefore are charged with love, are charged with God and if we know how to touch them give off sparks and take fire, yield drops and flow, ring and tell of him" (S, 195). And what of breath? Surely as careful a Latinist as Hopkins would have been alive to the etymological connection between "breath" and "inspiration." The shortness of breath that yields only sighs is Hopkins's confession of his weakness of poetic style. His poems lack inspiration; he cannot breathe any life into them. They are perpetually out of breath. "To R. B." is, literally and figuratively, Hopkins's last gasp as a poet.

What makes this poem so extraordinarily moving is its frank confession of failure in tones and rhythms of controlled sorrow. One might cite this poem, along with "Thou art indeed just, Lord" and "My own heart let me have more pity on" and the closing lines of "That Nature is a Heraclitean Fire," as exemplary instances of the resignation and spiritual peace attained by Hopkins in his final years. Such an interpretation would, of course, be difficult to sustain in the face of the letters and the retreat notes of 1888 and 1889, but even if we confine ourselves to the poetry, this manner of reading Hopkins's late work is not entirely satisfactory. For what does it mean for a poet to be resigned? What does resignation yield in poetic terms? "To R. B." eloquently testifies to the high price paid by the poet for having withdrawn from the struggle toward an original style, his having resigned himself to a life without poetry. What the poet resigns is his poetic career, the sign of which is his loss of the ability to create, to produce, to beget poems. As Hillis Miller, Edward Said, and others have persuasively shown, the characteristic metaphors of Hopkins's later career indicate his consciousness of his sterility, his lack of fecundity, even his impotence. In the octet of "To R. B.," Hopkins indicates the figural relationship of inspiration to poetry in a sexual conceit:

> The fine delight that fathers thought; the strong
> Spur, live and lancing like the blowpipe flame,
> Breathes once and, quenchèd faster than it came,
> Leaves yet the mind a mother of immortal song.
>
> Nine months she then, nay years, nine years she long
> Within her wears, bears, cares and combs the same:
> The widow of an insight lost she lives, with aim
> Now known and hand at work now never wrong.

Behind this striking imagery of fecundation lies the mystery of the Annunciation, the impregnation of Mary by the Holy Spirit at the moment of Gabriel's uttering: "Hail, full of grace, the Lord is with thee. Blessed art thou among women" (Luke 1: 28). Hopkins likens the poet's momentary inspiration to the instant of conception and suggests that the power of this briefly flickering flame is such as to engender, even years later, the birth of poetry. But Hopkins himself cannot produce poems any longer, having been abandoned by the "Sweet fire the sire of muse." His poetry lacks that "strong spur" which fertilizes the mind's womb. In his essay on "the question of style" in Nietzsche, Jacques Derrida has elucidated the metaphor of the spur as a figure for literary style, with all the masculine, "phallogocentric" force that this figure carries.[5] Similarly, Hopkins figuratively imagines poetic fire and breath—which are themselves already figural representations of poetry, figures of the irreducibly figurative, one might say—as "spurred" into being by the masculine spirit of "delight." Poetry is animated (the etymological pun is apt) by the procreative joy of the inspired poet. The absence of such joy or sexual energy is the signature of sorrow, the confession of impotence, the diminished greatness of "To R. B." Hopkins's resignation constitutes, not merely acceptance of death as inevitable, but his withdrawal from creative life. In "To R. B." Hopkins condemns himself to death as a poet; he signs the death warrant that typhoid was to seal only a few weeks later.

This bleak and sad moment in "To R. B." was preceded by an intense struggle to remain alive poetically. Hopkins's last period was his most glorious, not for the poetic successes he achieved, but for the futility he so passionately strove to overcome. Few poets have struggled so valiantly against the ebbing of their poetic energies, and even fewer have managed to erect such singularly grand monuments to their failure.

"Carrion Comfort" and the four "terrible sonnets" that follow it are a kind of purgation for Hopkins. In them he dramatizes his continuing fight to remain a poet, and through them he is able to "father-forth" the three great and truly Hopkinsian poems of his last period, "Tom's Garland," "Harry Ploughman," and "That Nature is a Heraclitean Fire and of the comfort of the Resurrection." But even in the latter three poems, Hopkins cannot entirely efface his consciousness of impending disaster, the awareness that he has perhaps given up too much to become a poet and that his loss is registered finally in the dying of his poetic fire. "Carrion Comfort" is, even for Hopkins, an extraordinarily physical

---

[5]Jacques Derrida, "La Question du style," in *Nietzsche aujourd'hui?* 2 vols. (Paris: Union Générale d'Editions, 1973), 1: 235-87.

poem. The images of twisting, bruising, wrestling, toiling, and threshing testify to the intensity of the spiritual struggle the poet undergoes. This brute physicality indicates the considerable vitality that remained in Hopkins's poetic will, however endangered and enfeebled it may have become. The poem opens with an energetic assertion of selfhood:

> Not, I'll not, carrion, comfort, Despair, not feast on thee;
> Not untwist—slack they may be—these last strands of man
> In me ór, most weary, cry *I can no more*. I can;
> Can something, hope, wish day come, not choose not to be. [P, 99]

The poem protests, it refuses, it resists, but all this in the negative mode. It is important to note the difference between the voice in these lines and the more positive, almost celebratory tone of the sonnets written shortly after "The Wreck of the Deutschland." "The world is charged with the grandeur of God," "Look at the stars! look, look up at the skies!," "Nothing is so beautiful as Spring— / When weeds, in wheels, shoot long and lovely and lush," "I caught this morning morning's minion," "Glory be to God for dappled things—," "Summer ends now; now, barbarous in beauty, the stooks, rise / Around"—how different, how affirmative, how joyous these opening lines sound in comparison to the first stanza of "Carrion Comfort." The earlier poems proclaim the triumph of the poet, his realization of his special style, his birth as a poet, while "Carrion Comfort" witnesses his diminished strength, his feeble attempt to "not choose not to be."

The second stanza turns from an assertion of will to complaint, to a Job-like questioning of the justice of the poet's affliction:

> But ah, but O thou terrible, why wouldst thou rude on me
> Thy wring-world right foot rock? lay a lionlimb against me?
>   scan
> With darksome devouring eyes my bruisèd bones? and fan
> O in turns of tempest, me heaped there; me frantic to avoid
>   thee and flee?

Gardner glosses "rude" as an adverbial form, now rare in English, meaning "rudely" (P, 287), but the submerged pun on "rood" is equally evident. Christ's suffering on the cross is, here as elsewhere in Hopkins, an important analogue to the mental anguish of the poet. And "rood" can also mean, according to the Oxford English Dictionary which cites an instance of such usage contemporary with Hopkins, "to spawn." The image of procreation involving struggle and pain recalls many similar

images in Hopkins's writings, particularly the sexual union and bringing
forth of the *Logos* by the tall nun in imitation of Mary in "The Wreck of
the Deutschland." Read in this way, the stanza is a lament over the
intensity and difficulty of bringing forth verse. Faced by the prospect of
the struggle, by the overwhelming burden of such a fate, the poet confesses
himself "frantic to avoid thee and flee." But who is this "thee" to whom
the stanza is addressed? The personification of Despair in the first stanza
leads one to believe that the second stanza is also addressed to this
allegorical adversary, rather like the personified abstraction Despair in
Book I of *The Faerie Queene.* But line nine seems to dispute this reading,
repeating the question "Why?" and answering: "That my chaff might fly;
my grain lie, sheer and clear." The conventional Christian symbol of
separating fruit from chaff suggests that the poem addresses God in the
second stanza and therefore represents Christian spirituality and the
plight of the soul struggling toward salvation.

This reading is valid, but to my mind it does not go quite far enough.
Here again, as in "To R. B.," "The Windhover," "The Wreck of the
Deutschland," and "Spelt from Sibyl's Leaves," the true subject of the
poem is the poet's inner battle, represented and realized in the poem
itself, to become a poet. Hopkins asks "O thou terrible, why wouldst
thou . . . scan / With darksome devouring eyes my bruisèd bones?"
"Scan" seems an odd word in this context, unless one reads the poem as
an allegory of poetry. The terrible being who opposes Hopkins is his own
poetic self, the most exacting and powerful of adversaries; the "bruisèd
bones" he scans are the lines of the poem. Scanning is inspection, observation, and also the search for rhythmical regularity. The "turns of tempest"
"fanned" over the "heaped" poet are those poetic storms that one encounters everywhere in Hopkins's poetry, but most powerfully in "The
Wreck of the Deutschland." But in the earlier poems, Hopkins's spiritual
anguish was turned into the successful realization of the poetic self. In
"Carrion Comfort," though the poem is produced, the final image is not
of reconciliation between poet and adversary, but of contention and the
inability of the poet to identify the true object of his poetry:

Nay in all that toil, that coil, since (seems) I kissed the rod,
Hand rather, my heart lo! lapped strength, stole joy, would
    laugh, chéer.
Cheer whom though? The hero whose heaven-handling flung
    me, fóot tród
Me? or me that fought him? O which one? is it each one?

>   That night, that year
> Of now done darkness I wretch lay wrestling with (my God!)
>   my God.

Hopkins's "cheering" is his poetic celebration, more fully achieved in "The Windhover," of the poet's identifying his vocation with Christ's Redemption. Another way of putting this is to say that the struggle to poetry which, in "The Windhover," was ultimately identified with the vocation of the soul as servant and imitator of Christ is, in "Carrion Comfort," opposed to the religious vocation. The poet is separated from and even at war with Christ over his destiny. His always fragile and endangered peace with his style is figuratively represented as the struggle between the individual soul and the strength of his divine calling. The poet wrestles with his personal god, that idealized image of himself as strong poet who wrenches the poet out of his facile stylistic regularities and compels him to write in a new idiom, which for Hopkins always meant a new rhythm. These last five lines are written in the past tense, and to some extent they are the recollection of a past personal and poetic crisis. But "Carrion Comfort" is written on the eve of a violent renewal of this crisis, so that the poem is both a repetition of the past and a prolepsis of what is to come. The poet's struggle with his style is never over, not until he abandons his ambition, which is always his fate, to be the creative, original fathering figure of distinctive verse.

Hopkins once wrote to Bridges concerning the sonnets that follow "Carrion Comfort," and what he says of them is as interesting as it is uncharacteristic of him:

> I shall shortly have some sonnets to send you, five or more. Four of these came like inspirations unbidden and against my will. And in the life I lead now, which is one of a continually jaded and harassed mind, if in any leisure I try to do anything I make no way—nor with my work, alas! but so it must be. [L. I, 221]

Hopkins rarely avers openly that his poems are written from inspiration, and he never admits in other cases that poetry comes to him "unbidden and against my will." Clearly, these poems represent something unusual, even extraordinary for Hopkins, though it might be better to say that they teach again the lesson the poet has learned before but must learn with each poem (or here with a new suite of poems): That he is never quite the master of his own style, of his poetic individuality, that poetry is always a compromise with the strong, resistant god who warps the poet's will and compels him to revise himself creatively or to give up the quest for originality.

Hopkins's commentators have observed that the five poems which succeed "Carrion Comfort" reveal a stylistic revision in Hopkins. Their diction has fewer archaisms and dialectical usages, their syntax is less tortured, their rhythms less difficult to determine. This stylistic simplicity seems odd at first, since the theme of these poems is the most rigorous and painful self-examination, and one might project a correspondingly tortured verse to represent the poet's tortured soul. Various reasons for such a stylistic revision in Hopkins have been advanced. Elisabeth Schneider cites the influence of Bridges and his poetry on Hopkins's late style from the time of "Andromeda" onward.[6] This is a suggestive hypothesis that I wish to modify a bit. While it may be true that Bridges exercised a certain influence over Hopkins's thinking, perhaps more than Hopkins himself might have wished, it is difficult to believe that a poet with Hopkins's strength of will and preternatural sense of selfhood could have been absorbed by the force of Bridges's style. Nevertheless, the merit of Elisabeth Schneider's hypothesis remains in that it shows Hopkins becoming, in some sense, a different poet in these poems, momentarily abandoning the strong, original style which had marked all his best poetry since "The Wreck of the Deutschland." But for a poet, giving up his strong poetic self is tantamount to giving up poetry, and this is precisely what these poems do. They prepare the way for Hopkins's abandonment, a gradual one accomplished over a period of some four years, of his poetic career. All Hopkins's great poems dramatize the poet's *askesis;* the singularity of his last poems is that this *askesis* comes finally to include poetry itself.

"No worst, there is none" is the diametric opposite of "Carrion Comfort," for it opens with an exclamation that negates the negative will of the first quatrain of the latter poem:

No worst, there is none. Pitched past pitch of grief,
More pangs will, schooled at forepangs, wilder wring.
Comforter, where, where is your comforting?

[6]See Elisabeth Schneider, *The Dragon in the Gate* (Berkeley and Los Angeles: University of California Press, 1968), pp. 126-43, 177-200.

> Mary, mother of us, where is your relief?
> My cries heave, herds-long; huddle in a main, a chief-
> woe, world-sorrow; on an age-old anvil wince and sing—
> Then lull, then leave off. [P, 100]

The "age-old anvil" recalls the powerful image of God's shaping will that opens the tenth stanza of "The Wreck of the Deutschland": "With an anvil-ding / And with fire in him forge thy will / Or rather, rather then, stealing as Spring / Through him, melt him but master him still" (P, 54). But in the later poem, the forging of verse does not occur, the "age-old anvil" that did once "wince and sing" can now only "lull, then leave off." The poem is not simply a complaint about the rigors of the poetic life; Hopkins is "pitched past pitch of grief." The poem announces the poet's retreat from the poetic life and his abandonment of the dangers of sublimity:

> O the mind, mind has mountains; cliffs of fall
> Frightful, sheer, no-man-fathomed. Hold them cheap
> May who ne'er hung there. Nor does long our small
> Durance deal with that steep or deep. Here! creep,
> Wretch, under a comfort serves in a whirlwind: all
> Life death does end and each day dies with sleep.

The shadow of Wordsworth and his successors in the Romantic tradition hangs heavily over these lines. No poet in English did more than Wordsworth to enshrine in the language the figure of the mind's mountains; no poet more successfully internalized nature and the quest for the poetic Sublime. Hopkins's greatest poem in this mode is "The Wreck of the Deutschland," but here he renounces the perils of the Sublime, having glimpsed the precariousness of its inspiration, and retreats into the comforting sleep of a less demanding poetic style. It is Hopkins's great insight in the final line to have understood that this sleep means death, the end of his poetic career. Only by daring to ascend the heights of poetic sublimity can the poet remain alive, creative, productive as a poet.

A difficult and painful insight results from this and from the majority of Hopkins's later poems, and it would be a mistake to ignore it in reading them. The opposition of poetic Sublime to poetic death just formulated is somewhat misleading, since the experience of the Sublime is precisely a confrontation with death and a denial of its ultimate power to silence the poet. The poetry of the Sublime ("The Wreck of the Deutschland") resists the inevitability of death and postpones it momentarily. But

the distinguishing feature of this and Hopkins's other late poems is their
acceptance of death, their refusal to renew the struggle against death and
their gradual fading into silence. Hopkins's acute insight into his own
poetic power made him understand that he was indeed dying, that he
could no longer muster the strength to stave off what for all men is
inevitable but what for creating poets remains unimaginable—the fact of
mortality. Hopkins's late poems register the extremity to which the poet
must be driven before accepting this fact.

The poet's waning energy to write is further anatomized in the next
two poems. Separated from his homeland, estranged from those surrounding him, Hopkins bemoans his lack of fecundity, which he attributed
to the deafness of his muse—here England—to his pleas:

> England, whose honour O all my heart woos, wife
> To my creating thought, would neither hear
> Me, were I pleading, plead nor do I: I wear-
> y of idle a being but by where wars are rife. [P, 101]

Gardner glosses this stanza and the next as references to the political
strife in Ireland in the 1880's. But if we read the sonnet from a political
perspective, what are we to make of the closing lines:

>   Only what word
> Wisest my heart breeds dark heaven's baffling ban
> Bars or hell's spell thwarts. This to hoard unheard,
> Heard unheeded, leaves me a lonely began.

Both Gardner and Father Peters read "began" as a verb intended as a
noun, meaning "beginner" or perhaps "beginning." I would read it as a
predicate with an understood "I" preceding. The significance of these
lines is Hopkins's melancholy realization that his poetry is "unheard,"
not only in the obvious sense that it remains unpublished, but also in the
more pressing circumstances of his immediate poetic life. The very words
themselves are beginning to fail him, and he is left with the mere husk of
poetic achievement, the consciousness merely that "I began." Hopkins is
increasingly convinced of the futility of his own writing, of the failure of
his language to become articulate. His figurative representation of this
pathetic state of mind depicts him among the damned in hell whose
prayers for deliverance from suffering go unheeded:

>   And my lament
> Is cries countless, cries like dead letters sent

To dearest him that lives alas! away.

I am gall, I am heartburn. God's most deep decree
Bitter would have me taste: my taste was me;
Bones built in me, flesh filled, blood brimmed the curse.

Selfyeast of spirit a dull dough sours. I see
The lost are like this, and their scourge to be
As I am mine, their sweating selves; but worse. [P, 101]

The poem is a "lament," but like the "unheeded word" of the previous poem, this verse "is cries countless, cries like dead letters sent." Hopkins's poems resemble those dead letters invoked by Melville at the end of "Bartleby": "On errands of life, these letters speed to death." Even more disturbing is that this futility and suffering originated in the poet himself. There seems no way out of the prison that the poet has constructed, no way except to be other than he is, to cease to be a poet, which is to cease to be at all.

In the next sonnet, Hopkins discovers there is a way to cope with his poetic destiny, though he does not minimize the difficulty of realizing this solution. Deliverance from mental turmoil comes with patience:

Patience, hard thing! the hard thing but to pray,
But bid for, Patience is! Patience who asks
Wants war, wants wounds; weary his times, his tasks;
To do without, take tosses, and obey. [P, 102]7

Patience is another form of the familiar *askesis* necessary to become a poet, though here passivity is the dominant note of the poet's mental state. It appears that if the poet can bear with the stressful time of his present affliction, if he can but be patient, he will emerge into a more calm, a more tolerable future state of the soul. But the remainder of the poem defeats this hopeful expectation:

Rare patience roots in these, and, these away,
Nowhere. Natural heart's ivy, Patience masks
Our ruins of wrecked past purpose. There she basks
Purple eyes and seas of liquid leaves all day.

We hear our hearts grate on themselves: it kills

7The inspiration for this sonnet on patience may well have been Milton's sonnet on his blindness, which invokes patience in reply to the poet's lament over his wasted "talent": "'Doth God exact day-labour, light denied,' / I fondly ask; But patience to prevent / That murmur, soon replies" (John Milton, *Complete Poems and Major Prose*, ed. Merritt Y. Hughes [Indianapolis: Bobbs, Merrill, 1957], p. 168).

To bruise them dearer. Yet the rebellious wills
Of us we do bid God bend to him even so.

And where is he who more and more distills
Delicious kindness?—He is patient. Patience fills
His crisp combs, and that comes those ways we know.

Patience does indeed offer relief from affliction, but only at the price of
the poet's ignoring the truth about himself. Patience requires a sublimation
(in the psychoanalytic sense of the term) of the poet's knowledge about
himself, a covering over or "masking" of his own failure, the "ruins of
wrecked past purpose." Patience is an evasion of the poet's destiny, for
though it alleviates the suffering of the poetic self grating and straining
against itself, it does so at the cost of the poet's creative energies.

Hopkins's "terrible sonnets" teach a melancholy double lesson: Poems
are written only at enormous psychic cost to the poet; Hopkins himself
can no longer bear such psychic expense. What issues from the dark night
of the poetic soul recorded in these poems is the registering of relief along
with the passive acceptance of God's grace that signals the abandonment
of Hopkins's personal struggle to be a poet:

My own heart let me more have pity on; let
Me live to my sad self hereafter kind,
Charitable; not live this tormented mind
With this tormented mind tormenting yet.

I cast for comfort I can no more get
By groping round my comfortless, than blind
Eyes in their dark can day or thirst can find
Thirst's all-in-all in all a world of wet.

Soul, self; come, poor Jackself, I do advise
You, jaded, let be; call off thoughts awhile
Elsewhere; leave comfort root-room; let joy size

At God knows when to God knows what; whose smile
's not wrung, see you; unforeseen times rather—as skies
Betweenpie mountains—lights a lovely mile. [P, 102-3]

Appropriately, this poem is the least twisted and contorted in rhythm
and syntax of all the sonnets written at this period of Hopkins's career.
Hopkins's desire to "not live this tormented mind / With this tormented
mind tormenting yet" yields the stylistic restraint of this poem, rivaled in
simplicity among Hopkins's major poems only by his final work,
"To R. B." He advises himself to give up the intensely introspective life

dramatized in his recent poems, but in so doing he effectively abandons that quest for self-realization that has been the theme and the creating force of all of his great poems. Poetry, as Hopkins has averred again and again in his own verse and prose, requires an act of will. The passivity of waiting for the grace of God to reveal unexpectedly moments of beauty and comfort may deliver Hopkins from his inner torment, but it will not help him to write poems. Hopkins's severe curtailment of his stylistic individuality in this poem is the effective limitation of his own poetic will. Spiritual comfort and stylistic clarity are purchased at the expense of the poet's creative strength.

The obvious rejoinder to the interpretation I have been developing is that Hopkins did not lapse into silence after this poem but continued to write and produced some of his finest verse, including "That Nature is a Heraclitean Fire." What are we to make of this burst of creativity, this apparent resuscitation of Hopkins's poetic will? And what to make of Hopkins's return, in "Tom's Garland," "Harry Ploughman," and "That Nature is a Heraclitean Fire," to the vigorous and characteristic sprung rhythms of his greatest verse and to the knotty syntax and lexical innovation which are the most distinctive features of his poetic style? Why and how does Hopkins succeed in resurrecting a style and a self that he had seemingly renounced and buried?

As I suggested in the introduction, the poetic scene of instruction is not a moment for all time; that is to say, the poet does not, in writing a poem, conclude once and for all his struggle with the demon of his poetic self. Each new poem returns to the same battleground for stylistic originality that previous poems had fought to master. The poet, in effect, has continually to rediscover what he has always known: to become a poet demands a ceaseless revision of himself, a rewriting of himself in each poem. Hopkins might have ceased to write poetry altogether after the experience of the "terrible sonnets"; that he did not cease merely shows how acutely he understood the paradoxical truth presented in those poems. Poetry is a psychic battleground where one achieves at best an uneasy truce with the demon of poetic creation. Poetry stops being written only with the physical or stylistic death of the poet. As Valéry once wisely remarked: "A poem is never finished; it is only abandoned."

The poems Hopkins wrote during the final two years of his life are works of compromise and finally of withdrawal. From "Tom's Garland" (September 1887) to his last sonnet dedicated to Bridges (April 1889), the

arc of his career records Hopkins's ultimate defeat as a poet, his painful
recognition that his personal quest for poetic sublimity has failed. It is
not coincidental that at this period Milton comes more and more to
haunt Hopkins. Throughout Hopkins's letters, references to Milton's
prosody and style are numerous and detailed. Along with Tennyson,
Milton is the most frequently discussed poet in the letters, and he seems
to have exercised a decisive influence over Hopkins's poetic practice from
"The Wreck of the Deutschland" onward. In his earlier explanations of
the origin of sprung rhythm, Hopkins had attributed his discovery to a
variety of sources, but most prominently to the choruses of *Samson
Agonistes* and certain sections of *Paradise Regained*.[8] In a letter to his
mother, Hopkins also professed the metrical influence of Milton on "God's
Grandeur" and "The Starlight Night" (L. III, 144). Hopkins associated
Milton most often with "plainness and severity," with a style, one might
say, the very antithesis of Hopkins's own. In 1879, he wrote to Bridges
and enclosed his sonnet "Andromeda," about which he commented: "I
endeavoured in it at a more Miltonic plainness and severity than I have
anywhere else. I cannot say it has turned out severe, still less plain, but it
seems almost free from quaintness and in aiming at one excellence I may
have hit another" (L. I, 87). The ideal of "Miltonic plainness" stood before
Hopkins from the beginning of his maturity as a poet, as he confessed in
the famous letter to Bridges on the "oddness" of his own style: "I hope in
time to have a more balanced and Miltonic style. But as air, melody, is
what strikes me most of all in music and design in painting, so design,
pattern or what I am in the habit of calling 'inscape' is what I above all
aim at in poetry. Now it is the virtue of design, pattern, or inscape to be
distinctive and it is the vice of distinctiveness to become queer. This vice I
cannot have escaped" (L. I, 66).[9] Milton represents for Hopkins an
antithetical self (in the exact sense of Yeats's term), the strong precursor
in whose shadow Hopkins always stood, but never more completely than
in the poems of his last two years of life.[10]

[8]See especially Hopkins's Preface to his poems (P, 46-47) and the letters to Bridges (L. I,
37-38, 156) and to Dixon (L. II, 13-15).

[9]Also noteworthy is the letter to Dixon in which Hopkins links Wordsworth and the
lake poets to Milton and identifies their stylistic affinities as "the mean or standard of
English style and diction" (L. II, 98).

[10]Elisabeth Schneider invokes Yeats's term in the final paragraph of her study of Hopkins,
though she believes that to employ it as a descriptive epithet for Hopkins's late style is a
distortion of Yeats's meaning. Harold Bloom, of course, has done much to make Yeats's
concept available for criticism, and I find no distortion of Yeats in employing the term to
describe Hopkins's poetic self in the late poems. Moreover, I think Ms. Schneider incorrectly
identifies Bridges as the influential figure on Hopkins's late plain style; Milton seems to me
the much more likely candidate for reasons that I shall enumerate shortly.

In November 1887, Hopkins wrote to Bridges requesting advice on
how to attach codas to a sonnet. Bridges responded, not entirely satis-
factorily, that the exemplary instance was Milton's "On the New Forcers
of Conscience," a fact Hopkins already knew. Hopkins thanked him for
his trouble, and then proceeded to discuss the obscurities of "Harry
Ploughman":

> I want Harry Ploughman to be a vivid figure before the mind's eye; if
> he is not that the sonnet fails. The difficulties are of syntax no doubt.
> Dividing a compound word by a clause sandwiched into it was a
> desperate deed, I feel, and I do not feel that it was an unquestionable
> success. . . . My meaning surely *ought* to appear of itself; but in a
> language like English, and in an age of it like the present, written
> words are really matter open and indifferent to the receiving of
> different and alternative verse-forms, some of which the reader cannot
> possibly be sure are meant unless they are marked for him. . . . One
> thing I am now resolved on, it is to prefix short prose *arguments* to
> some of my pieces. These too will expose me to carping, but I do not
> mind. Epic and drama and ballad and many, most, things should be
> at once intelligible; but everything need not and cannot be. Plainly if
> it is possible to express a sub[t]le and recondite thought on a subtle
> and recondite subject in a subtle and recondite way and with great
> felicity and perfection, in the end, something must be sacrificed, with
> so trying a task, in the process, and this may be the being at once,
> nay perhaps even the being without explanation at all, intelligible.
> [L. I, 265-66]

Hopkins's precedent for prefixing "short prose arguments" to his poetry
surely must have been *Paradise Lost*, the most famous example in English
of this device. Hopkins's contorted argument in this passage can be
attributed to his divided sense of himself as a poet. Though he wishes to
be understood, to achieve "Miltonic plainness," he also knows that his
own strength as a poet lies elsewhere, in precisely the obscurities of
syntax that he confesses made "Harry Ploughman" a failure. Hopkins is
trapped in what Harold Bloom has called the anxiety of influence, the
paradoxical situation of the modern poet in which he is compelled to
honor and to imitate his precursors and to differ from them at the same
time: "The effect of studying masterpieces is to make me admire and do
otherwise. So it must be on every original artist to some degree, on me to
a marked degree" (L. I, 291).

Some months later, Hopkins expressed the same apprehension about
the failure of his style in "Tom's Garland":

I laughed outright and often, but very sardonically, to think you and the Canon could not construe my last sonnet; that he had to write to you for a crib. It is plain I must go no farther on this road: if you and he cannot understand me who will? Yet, declaimed, the strange constructions would be dramatic and effective. Must I interpret it? [L. I, 272]

Hopkins's lengthy explication of the sonnet concludes on a sad, weary note: "And I think that it is a very pregnant sonnet and in point of execution very highly wrought. Too much so, I am afraid" (L. 1, 274). The poem itself makes an ironic contrast between the mental life of a common laborer, largely free from care, and the mental anguish of men like Hopkins himself:

Tom Heart-at-ease, Tom Navvy: he is all for his meal
Sure, 's bed now. Low be it: lustily he his low lot (feel
That ne'er need hunger, Tom; Tom seldom sick,
Seldomer heartsore; that treads through, prickproof, thick
Thousands of thorns, thoughts) swings though. [P, 103]

As Hopkins glosses this section: "But this place [the low station of the day laborer] still shares the common honour, and if it wants one advantage, glory or public fame, makes up for it by another, ease of mind, absence of care; and these things are symbolized by the gold and the iron garlands. (O, once explained, how clear it all is!)" (L. I, 273). The clarity that Hopkins desires and fails to achieve corresponds to the simplicity of the mental life of the laborer who is the central image in the poem. Through its obscurity and stylistic difficulty the poem produces the irreducible difference between the poet and the common laborer. Hopkins's greatest strength, his poetic idiosyncrasy, here becomes his most glaring weakness. The suffering and impotent poet represents the exact antithesis of the vigorous day-laborer. The same antithesis lies behind "Harry Ploughman" and is further elaborated in Hopkins's penultimate poem, "The shepherd's brow, fronting forked lightning":

The shepherd's brow, fronting forked lightning, owns
The horror and the havoc and the glory
Of it. Angels fall, they are towers, from heaven—a story
Of just, majestical, and giant groans.
But man—we, scaffold of score brittle bones;
Who breathe, from groundlong babyhood to hoary
Age gasp; whose breath is our *memento mori*—
What bass is *our* viol for tragic tones?

He! Hand to mouth he lives, and voids with shame;
And, blazoned in however bold the name,
Man Jack the man is, just; his mate a hussy.
And I that die these deaths, that feed this flame,
That . . . in smooth spoons spy life's masque mirrored: tame
My tempests there, my fire and fever fussy. [P, 107]

Contrasting shepherd and poet, Hopkins revises the pastoral tradition in which the two are identical. In this poem, the shepherd resembles the day-laborer of "Tom's Garland" and Harry Ploughman in his facing and coping with the disasters and sublimity of nature. The poet, whose song responds to the same figure of lightning across the sky, is out of tune with the "tragic tones" "fronted" so naturally by the shepherd. Hopkins's familiar metonymies for poetry, fire, breath, storm, and music, all occur in the poem, but in each case the trope has reversed its customary valency and now signifies the poet's diminished powers. An earlier version of the final two lines makes the point more blatantly: "In spoons have seen my masque played and how tame / My tempest and my spitfire freaks how fussy" (P, 297). Hopkins's "spitfire freaks," his explosive and fiery poems, have been tamed. "The horror and the havoc and the glory" (we might say the sublimity), those qualities so admirably captured in "The Wreck of the Deutschland," are absent from the poet's song. Here again, Milton stands behind Hopkins's estimation of the power of poetry, for the "horror and the havoc and the glory" of the fallen angels in the first book of *Paradise Lost* is the "story / Of just, majestical, and giant groans" to which Hopkins alludes in the third and fourth lines. The true subject of the poem is the Sublime, the poetic mode most successfully mastered in English by Milton but no longer within Hopkins's grasp. The tempestuous glory of "The Wreck of the Deutschland" has been transformed into mere rhetorical "fussiness." Hopkins's breath, his inspiration, is slowly dying; each new poem is but a feeble gasp, a pathetic *"memento mori."*

Even in "That Nature is a Heraclitean Fire and of the comfort of the Resurrection," his last, most vigorous effort to resuscitate his earlier style, which Elisabeth Schneider appropriately labels "baroque," the impulse toward jubilation and revel characteristic of the earlier nature sonnets is replaced by a severe curtailment of the poet's self-presentation. Though "million-fuelèd, | nature's bonfire burns on," the poet himself is all but burned out:

> Million-fuelèd, | nature's bonfire burns on.
> But quench her bonniest, dearest | to her, her clearest-selvèd
>   spark
> Man, how fast his firedint, | his mark on mind, is gone!
> Both are in an unfathomable, all is in an enormous dark
> Drowned. O pity and indig | nation! Manshape, that shone
> Sheer off, disseveral, a star, | death blots black out; nor mark
>   Is any of him at all so stark
> But vastness blurs and time | beats level. [P, 105]

The poem is a reprise of Hopkins's career as a poet, alluding to the major figures he has adopted for his poetic style, figures at once traditional and yet made peculiarly Hopkins's own. Hopkins's drowning mind is resuced by the "comfort of the Resurrection"; his poetic ashes are redeemed in the miraculous transformation of Christ from "Jack, joke, poor potsherd" into "immortal diamond":

>   ' Across my foundering deck shone
> A beacon, an eternal beam. | Flesh fade, and mortal trash
> Fall to the residuary worm; | world's wildfire, leave but ash;
>   In a flash, at a trumpet crash
> I am all at once what Christ is, | since he was what I am, and
> This Jack, joke, poor potsherd, | patch, matchwood, immortal
>   diamond,
>   Is immortal diamond. [P, 105-6]

All commentators on this poem have noticed the importance of the imagery of transformation, but no one to my knowledge has seen that the transformation represented in the closing lines is a melancholy one for the poet, that the poem is about the death of the poet's special fire, of his poetic self. Like all the works of Hopkins's last period, this poem is not a celebration of poetic transfiguration but a confession of the poet's abandonment of poetry. The tone is not celebratory but elegiac; the poem invokes the state of ceaseless transformation which is the life of poetry while acknowledging the poet's ("This Jack, joke, poor potsherd") own resignation and submission to the end of such transformations in himself. As Hopkins well knows, the poet who has become "immortal diamond" has reached the end of the line.

The four poems composed after "That Nature is a Heraclitean Fire" are all confessions of failure written in the antithetical plain style Hopkins associated with Milton. The sonnet on St. Alphonsus Rodriguez is virtually a rewriting of Milton's sonnet on his blindness, though unlike the poem on patience which had also invoked the same Milton sonnet, this poem is neither comforting nor consoling. When Milton wrote "They also serve who only stand and wait," his greatest poetry lay before him; but Hopkins knew that his greatest poems had already been written, that the saint who "in Majorca . . . watched the door" represents the poet whose voice has gone unheeded and whose career is about to end. The poet here is the antithesis of himself in "The Windhover," as the octet seems to echo and to invert the imagery of the earlier poem:

> Honour is flashed off exploit, so we say;
> And those strokes once that gashed flesh or galled shield
> Should tongue that time now, trumpet now that field,
> And, on the fighter, forge his glorious day.
> On Christ they do and on the martyr may;
> But be the war within, the brand we wield
> Unseen, the heroic breast not outward-steeled,
> Earth hears no hurtle then from fiercest fray. [P, 106]

The poet's *askesis*, figuratively represented by the doorkeeper saint, is realized in the stylistic restraint he practices here and in the poems that follow. In imitating Milton, Hopkins achieves a goal he had long cherished but had at the same time wished to postpone. By capitulating to Milton's example, Hopkins ceases to be himself. Just as St. Alphonsus's life is a feeble imitation of the lives of the martyrs and of Christ, so Hopkins's poetry has become a feeble imitation of Milton.

The last poems of Hopkins evoke the Miltonic specter who dominates and finally subdues them. Milton provides the model for the caudated sonnet form in "That Nature is a Heraclitean Fire," the theme of patience and willing subservience in "St. Alphonsus Rodriguez" and in the sonnet on patience, and the exemplary style of "plainness and severity" characteristic of much of Hopkins's later poetry. The creative revisionism of Milton and of the Romantic Sublime realized in "The Wreck of the Deutschland" has diminished to the lifeless repetitions of the last sonnets. Hopkins's life-long battle to achieve and sustain an original poetic style ends in the silent waiting of St. Alphonsus and the barely audible sigh of explanation that ends "To R. B." For Hopkins, the successful poet has always been a warrior, not unlike the soldier presented by Wallace Stevens at the end of "Notes Toward a Supreme Fiction." Hopkins also resembles Stevens in performing the extreme *askesis*, characteristic of so much modern poetry since Wordsworth, which denies the poet's exuberant celebration of himself and of nature and which makes of poetic excess and sublimity a tempting but forbidding demon. Hopkins's "winter world" figures forth the winter landscape of the modern poem presented in Stevens's "The Snow Man," just as Hopkins himself becomes at the end of his career the "mind of winter" that is a modern poet's ideal:

> One must have a mind of winter
> To regard the frost and the boughs
> Of the pine-trees crusted with snow;
>
> And have been cold a long time
> To behold the junipers shagged with ice,
> The spruces rough in the distant glitter
>
> Of the January sun; and not to think
> Of any misery in the sound of the wind,
> In the sound of a few leaves,
>
> Which is the sound of the land
> Full of the same wind
> That is blowing in the same bare place
>
> For the listener, who listens in the snow,
> And, nothing himself, beholds
> Nothing that is not there and the nothing that is.[11]

The drama of this poetry about nothing, played out in the stark landscapes of twentieth-century poets, is significantly and poignantly presaged in the career of Gerard Manley Hopkins. With him modern English poetry properly begins.

[11]Wallace Stevens, *The Collected Poems of Wallace Stevens* (New York: Alfred A. Knopf, 1954), pp. 9-10.

INDEX